To Arni

with much appreciation &

friendship.

Colombo   2 III 2542

Global Healing

Global Healing

Essays and Interviews on Structural Violence
Social Development and Spiritual Transformation

by

Sulak Sivaraksa

Thai Inter-Religious Commission for Development
Sathirakoses-Nagapradipa Foundation
Bangkok

Thai Inter-Religious Commission for Development
Sathirakoses-Nagapradipa Foundation
124 Soi Wat Thongnopphakhun, Somdej Chao Phya Road, Klongsarn
Thonburi, BKK. 10600
ISBN : 974-260-156-9

Printed at Ruankaew Printing House, Bangkok, Thailand

Edited by Michael Sheehy and Chris Walker

Jacket and book design by Song Sayam Co., Ltd.
Front page :   photograph of Avalokitasavara Bodhisattva from Chaiya, Southern
Siam, which is now in the National Museum, Bangkok. The
Bodhisattva is the personification of the Buddha's Compassion,
which could really be a global healing.
Cartoons at back cover and on page 166 : by Wallop Manyam
Drawing at frontispiece : by Tom Welsh
Photographs at the two flaps : by Prasitthiporn Karn-onsri
Front flap :   the author with H.H. the Dalai Lama and the Secretary-General of
Amnesty International in Paris 10th December 1998 to mark the 50th
anniversary of the Universal Declaration of Human Rights.
Back flap: Soothing spirit for the author by members of the Assembly of the
Poor, after he was arrested in March 1998.

Sulak Sivaraksa
Global Healing: Essays and Interviews on Structural Violence, Social
Development and Spiritual Transformation

US$ 15.-
ราคา ๔๕๐ บาท

Distributed by Suksit Siam: 113-115 Fuangnakorn Rd., Bangkok 10200
Fax: 662-222-5188, email: sop@ffc.or.th
Distributed in USA by Parallax Press: P.O.Box 7355, Berkeley, Cal.94707
Fax: 1-510-525-7129, www.parallax.org
Distributed in UK by Green Books: Food House, Hartland, Bidetard, Devon
EX396EE
Distributed in Australia by Mandala Books: P.O.Box 8111 Camberwell North,
Victoria 3124, Australia
Ph. (03) 9882-2484, F. (03) 9882-2440, email: 100244.2755@compuserve.com

CONTENTS

Respectfully dedicated to

Mr. Karuna & Mrs. Ruang-urai Kusalasaya

They are good examples for Siamese Buddhist householders.
The only couple who together have tirelessly brought the best of the
messages of ancient and modern India to the awareness of
contemporary Siam during the last five decades.
They have thus fostered the Thai public to be able to trace
the roots of our wisdom to the land of Lord Buddha.
This wisdom is still relevant in Global Healing
if we know how to apply it skillfully.
Mr. Karuna Kusalasaya has written an endearing
English language biography, Life Without A Choice.
Despite the sufferings and obstacles he has faced in serving his
motherland, he has expressed them in a graceful way,
nonviolently and with forgiveness.

FOREWORD

When I agreed to write a foreword for Arjan Sulak Sivaraksa's book, **Global Healing**, I thought it would be a simple task. But when I went through the texts of the essays and interviews, and sat down to write, I saw how hard a task I had accepted. I found it hard because of the vastness of the canvas that the collection covers, as well as the depth of introspection and experience that is reflected in the texts that have been brought together. Sulak has addressed the crucial questions of our times with characteristic wisdom and authenticity. His profound spiritual training and insights, and his courageous social activism have combined to give him a unique understanding of what afflicts us today, and what we have to do to heal ourselves.

We are on the threshold of a new century. The century that is ending has been truly momentous in many ways. It has witnessed an incredible increase in our knowledge of the universe in which we live. This knowledge has increased our power. Power can be used to end suffering, to liberate the human being, and to enable self-fulfilment. It can also be used to create and perpetuate inequality, to achieve hegemony, to destroy, and to thwart the development and self-fulfilment of others.

Power is only a means. It can be used to achieve objectives that are beneficial to mankind, or injurious and suicidal. We have therefore to be wise in choosing our objectives as well as in retaining the ability to control the power that we generate or acquire.

An increase in power calls for at least commensurate increase in wisdom and restraint. Restraint must include self-restraint as well as the restraint of those who are vested with power by those who generate and delegate power. The objectives of social structures and institutions and the processes that are used should therefore be such as preserve and promote this restraint. The moment we look upon power as an end in itself, we enter the vicious cycle of suppression, exploitation, domination, aggrandizement, violence, and retaliatory violence. Our objective then becomes not merely the acquistion of power but also the retention of power in our hands. We are ready to use any means that we can employ to ensure control over power. We look for subtle and ingenious ways of ensuring our hegemony. We fashion institutions that legitimize subtle, and systemic or structural, violence and demand the right to use violence against those who dissent or groups that stand in the way of our designs or ambitions or contentions. Such a configuration makes it impossible for individual human beings or groups of human beings to live in peace and harmony, and to seek development and fulfilment according to their own rights.

No elaborate statistics or arguments are necessary to prove that we have not used power with wisdom or compassion; that we have not preserved or promoted the restraint that makes power a good servant.

No one who believes in equality can deny that compassion is as much a social imperative as an ethical imperative.

That we have not given evidence of much wisdom is evident from the fact that our actions have given rise to two major threats to the survival of humanity. Firstly, we have manufactured and stock-piled weapons of mass destruction that can lead to the extinction of the human species, and the destruction of the environment on which all life depends. Secondly, we have evolved and employed a technology that depends on the profligate depletion of irreplacable resources, and leads to the poisoning of the air, water and earth on which all life depends. In the field of production as well as destruction, we have employed a technology that has taken us to the brink of suicide or self-inflicted destruction. We have employed it without fore-thought or fore-knowledge about the consequences and chain reactions that the materials and processes may have on our bodies, minds, social institutions, values and environment. This is not a sign of wisdom.

In support of technology, it is argued that it is the route to "development" and progress; that development is economic development; that economic development depends on the maximization and diversification of production; that maximization of production can be achieved only through a system that maximizes profit; that maximization of production in turn would lead to maximization of employment and to the elimination of poverty—to higher standards of living.

Experience has belied all these claims. In spite of the availability of resources and technology, in spite of the power to eliminate poverty and hunger, millions of human beings are dying of starvation and under-nourishment. Millions have no safe drinking water, no roof for shelter, no education, no protection from curable and communicable diseases. Those who have power and wealth live in affluence and profligacy, while the vast majority of humanity lives in want and fear. The technology that we use has only increased disparities between individual and individual, group and group, one area and another, within the country as well as on the globe. The seeds of disparity and injustice seem to be inherent in technology and the systems that has evolved from technology. This technology has not been used to or designed for the benefit of all. It has been used to serve the interests of those who seek power, profit and self-indulgence. It has been a subtle agent of elitism and exploitation. Whatever benefits a few without benefiting others, or at the cost of others, is bound to result in injustice, resentment and social conflict. It cannot be an instrument of peace or true development.

The current situation therefore raises many legitimate questions : who should benefit from the use of common resources and collective social effort—all, or a few? What should be our priorities in achieving development? Who should determine these priorities? Who should determine the values on which these priorities are formulated? What should be the processes through which these decisions or choices are made? What is the method that is being employed to brain-wash people into believing that the choices and decisions that govern "modern" technology were made to promote the interests of the common human being? What are the "sanctions" or means of constraint that have been used by the beneficiaries of the system to defraud the common human being? What are the means by which these sanctions can be countered, and the priorities altered? What are the means by which the individual and the system can be changed into something that truly transforms, liberates, and enriches the life of the common human being? What can common human beings do, individually and collectively, to bring about the transformation?

It is Sulak's view, and many of us will agree with him, that the grave crisis that humanity is facing today is our own creation;

human beings can therefore lead themselves out of the crisis. This can be done only if we decipher the causes of the crisis, and make up our minds to remove them. The prime cause is our unconcern for the law of cause and effect, and other laws that govern nature, human society, and the human mind. Nothing desirable, beneficial and durable can be built if we act in violation of these laws.

Mere maintenance of an animal existence or pampering of the body cannot be an adequate objective for the human being. The human being is more than the body. Any objective that ignores this unique nature of the human being cannot be worthy of the human being, cannot lead to his or her full or true development. Any process that does not give the mind and the spirit of man adequate scope for development and expression is inadequate and unworthy of the human being or a system which the human being fashions for his development. Material conditions are enabling conditions and cannot become ends in themselves. Materialism and consumerism cannot therefore serve as vehicles that can take us to the development of what is unique in the human being. They can only take us to the quagmire of titilation and discontent. The nature of desire is such that there is no sense of satiation even when one pays the penalty for indulgence.

The universe and all beings that live in it, exist within the paradigms of inter-dependence. This is all the more true of human beings, since the human species are gregarious and depend on each other for survival and progress. A little reflection will tell us that one of the paradigms that we cannot alter is that of inter-dependence or inter-being.

Where there is inter-dependence, there can be no irreconcilable conflict of interests. Apparent irreconcilability is the result of a false and distorted perception of the self, particularly as something that exists independently and inherently. If I hurt another, I hurt myself or at least a part of myself. If I want to advance, I have to advance in company. There is no growth that is possible at the cost of another. If I love myself, I must love others. Such love is the bond of cohesion that holds society, humanity, or the world together—because not merely life, but all phenomena are inter-related. We are as much part of the environment as the environment is a part of us. As His Holiness the Dalai Lama has pointed out, self-interest itself has to be "enlightened" self interest, if it is to serve one in any way.

What exists and thrives on the basis of inter-dependence cannot survive on the basis of competition. Competition and inter-dependence are not complementary; they are contradictory. It is altruism and co-operation that are consistent with inter-dependence, and not competition. An economic system that is based on competition, greed, and a form of technology that is designed to serve these is bound to lead to centralization, exploitation, cannibalization, globalization, consumerism and violence to protect the system.

Neither greed nor violence conforms to the paradigms of an inter-dependent society. Violence, whether it is implicit and structural or explicit cannot serve as a force of cohesion or transformation. It can only lead to annihilation or destruction. The pursuit of greed can only cause mental unrest in the individual. It cannot lead to satisfaction. It can only be pursued at the cost of the legitimate interest of others. It is therefore anti-social in intent as well as effect. Neither greed nor violence can lead to peace in the mind of the individual or in social relationships. They can only lead to anti-social indulgence and aggrandizement.

Buddha Dharma teaches us to avoid violence, greed, egoism and aggrandizement, and to build social institutions and relationships on the basis of the sense of inter-being, compassion, love and altruistic co-operation. It teaches that human beings cannot escape responsibility for their actions—of omission and commission. It teaches us to avoid what causes suffering and misery, to us and to others. It teaches us to accept responsibility for eliminating the causes of misery, and transforming ourselves and human society. One who believes in Buddha Dharma cannot escape this responsibility or acquience in the present dispensation which is based on greed and violence.

Sulak has explained how Dharma matters in every day life, how the light of Dharma can lead humanity out of the crisis that it has created for itself. I have greatly benefited by reading his exposition of what Dharma can do for the transformation of the individual and society and what those who believe in Dharma have to do today. I have no doubt many others will benefit in the same way as I have.

Ravindra Varma
President
Gandhi Peace Foundation, New Delhi

I will give you a talisman. Whenever you are in doubt, or when the self becomes too much with you, apply the following test:

Recall the face of the poorest and the weakest man whom you may have seen, and ask yourself, if the step you contemplate is going to be of any use to him. Will he gain anything by it? Will it restore him to a control over his own life and destiny? In other words, will it lead to swaraj for the hungry and spiritually starving millions? Then you will find your doubt and yourself melting away.

M.K. Gandhi

ACKNOWLEDGEMENTS

During the past few years I have often been asked to prepare papers for local, regional and international seminars or symposia, besides giving public lectures in Thai and English—not to mention interviews at home and abroad. Most of my English words were usually published in our journal *Seeds of Peace* as well as in the *Bangkok Post* and *The Nation*. Some magazines abroad like *Resurgence* in England and *Gandhi Marg* in India as well as *Tricycle* in the US and *Shambala Sun* in Canada sometimes published my English articles too; others were either translated from my English or Thai writings into French, Dutch, Italian, German, Portugese and Japanese.

As the written and spoken words were used on different occasions, they are bound to be repetitive, yet Michael Sheeny, formerly of the Naropa Institute, Boulder, Colorado, kindly read through them all and suggested some of the articles could be put together as a new volume, and he offered a very interesting title—*Global Healing: essays and interviews on structural violence, social development and spiritual transformation.*

Chris Walker, another Naropa alumnus, also helped to see that the book was properly edited. Roger Wheeler kindly agreed to review the manuscript for me before publication. Yet he helped to improve it tremendously.

Besides the above three gentlemen, quite a number of Buddhist friends helped drafting, editing, or polishing my English, especially Jane Rasbash, Jonathan Watts, David Arnott—to name but a few.

I am grateful to the various interviewers, editors and publishers, who first published the articles and allowed them to be reprinted in this volume. I am also thankful to those who invited me to speak at several places.

Among my Thai colleagues, I should like to thank Ms. Ladda Wiwarsurawech, Mrs. Thongtip Sutthakorn, Mr. Thamrong Patamapas, Mr. Nibond Chamduang, Ms. Sujintana Wangsakan and Mr. Pipop Udomittipong, as well as Ms. Nalinee Chunreong and Mr. Arsa Nattraibhop for their collaboration and patience.

It is indeed an honor to have Ravindra Varma, another fellow Buddhist from India, write the Foreword.

On my 65th birthday, Parallax Press kindly produced *Loyalty Demands Dissent: An Autobiography of An Engaged Buddhist.* This new volume is to be published on my 66th birthday, 27th March 1999. In the Buddhist reckoning, once one reaches the age of 66, one is really old. Perhaps from then on there may be words of wisdom from me for a change—if I manage to become less active and more contemplative. Ideally, one should combine inner strength with outward activities skilfully. I have tried to balance these two elements for the past few decades, but have experienced more failure than success.

Sulak Sivaraksa
14th December 1998

EDITOR' S INTRODUCTION

As we enter a new millenium, and the forces of materialism, egoism and consumerism run rampantly throughout societies, humanity is faced with concerns about the current order of the world and the uncertainty of its future. Our twentieth century has been an era of tremendous scientific and political advancements as well as a period of severe environmental and social degredation. The globalization of capitalism, the colonialization of corporations, and the industrialization of nations have begun to homogenize humanity and commercialize values. In our world, where people are enslaved for sex and exploited for labor, where violence is institutionalized, where mother earth is raped of her resources—we are confronted with the predicament of healing ourselves.

From the Buddhist perspective, social conditions of suffering originate from a delusory notion of the self. Buddha taught that the self is not an isolated entity that acts independently of its environment. He suggested that the self is a conscious process that acts interdependently with all physical and psychic phenomena. The difference between these two concepts of self is the difference between a rock and a river. A rock remains fixated in its bed of soil regardless of the winds that pass or the animals that range over it, a river flows unceasingly; a rock can exist alone, a river invites people and animals to bathe and drink. A river is analogous to the concept of self taught by the Buddha; it is an active stream that indefinitely affects its surroundings.

The Buddhist concept of self suggests that each action of an individual's body, speech and mind affects our world. Just as the pulse of your heart affects each cell of your body, your actions affect each sentient being. Once we consider the efficacy of our actions, it becomes apparent that we shape our world and our world shapes us. This means that we are responsible for our personal and social conditions and that we have the power to individually and collectively transform our condition.

During the last thirty years, there has been an escalating interest among activists and scholars about how to apply the Buddhist philosophy of liberation to personal, inter-personal and social transformation. Along with this interest, there has been an emerging tide of Buddhist liberation movements throughout South and Southeast Asia as well as America that emphasize the conjunction of political and spiritual practice to transform social conflicts. Engaged Buddhist movements assert that it is essential to place a dual emphasis on the cultivation of inner peace through spiritual practice with the cultivation of world peace through becoming actively involved in educational, cultural and political mediums to reduce global injustice.

One of the preeminent promulgators of the Buddhist philosophy of social transformation and a central figure in the engaged Buddhist movement is Sulak Sivaraksa. Sulak is a soft stout man who sits and listens with the silent attention of an owl and walks and speaks with the assurance of a Siamese tiger. For the last thirty-five years, he has been persecuted and praised for raising his voice for the sake of silenced voices throughout our world. In 1976, his books were burned and he was forced into exile for two years during Siam's bloodiest pro-democracy demonstrations. In 1984, he was arrested for criticizing the king in his book *Unmasking Thai Society*. He was arrested again in 1991 for a speech on the "Regression of Democracy in Siam" at Thammasat University, Bangkok. Although Sulak has been reprimanded for speaking out against corruption, he has also been awarded for his courage. He has been nominated for the Nobel Peace Prize and was the recipient of the Right Livelihood Award in 1995. Sulak has been successful in reviving and implementing socially engaged aspects of Buddhism and is a tireless advocate of justice because he is convinced that nonviolence is the only path to peace and that the human heart can be trusted.

In his native land of Siam, Sulak plays myriad roles including scholar, teacher, publisher, author and activist, but whatever mask he wears, Sulak is intuitively a critic. He questions society as Buddha encouraged his disciples to question the validity of his teachings. The Buddha warned his disciples that they would increase their ignorance if they naively welcomed his words without examining the truthfulness of his teachings. He compared the critical analysis required by a spiritual aspirant to the examination of gold by a goldsmith. As a goldsmith scrupulously inspects the purity and quality of a piece of gold, Sulak examines society and suggests ways to polish its taints and tarnishes.

In this book, *Global Healing: Essays and Interviews on Structural Violence, Social Development and Spiritual Transformation*, Sulak examines violence as a socially engineered phenomena, the effects of industrial development, and the spiritual role of an activist in transforming society. These writings, speeches and interviews probe into the hegemonic patterns of society and offer means to transform the existing structures that exacerbate social conflicts. Sulak's proposals are crucially important to anyone who wishes to understand the complexities of society or to anyone who feels compelled to transform society because he recognizes that it is "the ordinary man on the street" who is shaping our world.

Michael Sheehy

PART I

SAVIOR FROM SIAM

Sulak Sivaraksa in conversation with Rukmini Sekhar

The jury acclaims Sulak 'for his vision, activism and spiritual commitment in the quest for a development process that is rooted in democracy, justice and cultural integrity'.

Sulak's significant contribution has been to invert the authoritarian-dominated meaning of being Thai and being Buddhist from that of being against change to its true and original form. He legitimized people outside the circle of power who are fighting for liberty and who are accumulating wisdom to fight against authoritarianism as being truly Thai Buddhist. He called into question the authoritarians' use of the meaning of being Thai and being Buddhist as being 'against change'.

From citation of the 1995 Right Livelihood Award.

Ask me who is shaping the course of history and
I will tell you that it is the ordinary man in the
street.

Sulak Sivaraksa

The first thing that struck me about the man on the dais was that here was someone who screamed courage and boldness. I had heard about the fiery social critic and activist from Siam and had gone to listen to his lecture. He was a smallish man, wearing loose blue trousers and a khadi kurta with the ease of an old India-hand. When he got up to speak, his words were at once biting as he lashed out against hegemonic patterns of development, and soft and gentle as he emphasised non-violence and compassion as the only way.

Tom Ginsburg, editor of Sivaraksa's book, **Seeds of Peace** describes the man thus, 'Sulak is a prominent and outspoken Thai social critic and activist. He is the natural product of the contradictions of contemporary Thai life—educated abroad... and his politics are at once culturally conservative and socially progressive. Sulak is a lawyer, a teacher, a scholar, a publisher, the founder of many organisations and the author of more than sixty books and monographs in both Thai and English. During the last three decades, he has been a constant irritant, a "professional gadfly" for Thai governments. University of California anthropologist Herbert Phillips describes Sulak as a "Thai institution, in a class by himself".

When he returned to Siam after nine years of studying, teaching and working in England and Wales, he founded the *Social Science Review*, which became Thailand's foremost intellectual magazine. During this time, he became deeply interested in grassroots development and in the 1970s, he became the central figure in a number of non-governmental organisations in Siam. In 1976, Siam experienced its bloodiest coup. Sulak's books were burnt and he was forced to remain in exile for two years. In 1984, he was arrested on charges of *lèse-majesté* or criticising the king, after his book *Unmasking Thai Society* was published. After a wave of international protests he was released. He was again arrested in September 1991 for a talk he gave at Thammasat University on 'The Regression of Democracy in Siam'. He went into hiding and had to go into exile again. Sulak is a practising Buddhist and his critique of society flows from this. Says Ginsburg, 'He is among a handful of leaders worldwide working to revive the socially engaged aspects of Buddhism.' Right now he is busy developing two new initiatives. The first is an international network on Alternatives to Consumerism and second, the development of a new college in Thailand called Spirit in Education Movement. In 1995, he received the Right Livelihood Award.

Sulak is convinced that real individual, familial, social and political change can only be brought about non-violently and in this he draws his deepest inspiration from the Buddhadharma and Mahatma Gandhi. We focused therefore on some issues on violence and non-violence.

Rukmini Sekhar: *You have been recognized all over the world for fusing the metaphysics of Buddhism with hands on social activism. Why didn't you become a monk? Is it because it may have come in the* *way of your 'worldly' activism?*

Sulak Sivaraksa: Indeed I was once a monk in my country. Most young people become monks once in their lives either for four months or four years. I was a monk for eighteen months when I was very young. But I didn't stay as one. You see, it was the time of the Second World War. I went to a Protestant and then to a Catholic school. When the War came, all schools were closed. They had to move out of Bangkok. I did not like school. My father asked me whether I would like to move out of Bangkok to a boarding school. I said no. So he said, since you have been educated in Christian schools all your life, why don't you join the monkhood. So I did, and I really liked it and never wanted to leave! But my father begged me, saying that when I grew up, fell in love, and wanted to get married and work in the world, then what would I do? Gradually, because of his pleas, I left the monkhood.

But is it not true that many Buddhist abbots in South East Asia are involved in social activism? You don't feel that taking on the robes is an impediment?

     No, in Buddhism, a monk or a lay person has at least two roles to play: the first is to transform oneself from a violent to a nonviolent person, to reduce greed and lust, and ultimately, to change ignorance to understanding and wisdom. This would then transform itself to a love which is not self-love. The second part is how to relate meaningfully to others, not exploiting oneself or others. 'Others' mean other human beings, animals, all sentient beings—trees, rivers and so on. Monks are sometimes more effective than lay people in some areas and vice versa.

     I would add that people who claim to be rational, scientific and logical—intellectuals and technocrats—can and should learn from ordinary people, from the Buddha, from Gandhi, from various spiritual traditions, tribal and other indigenious societies. One can't help society without helping oneself. How can you help if you are angry, violent and impatient? So, in order to take care of others, one first has to take care of oneself.

But isn't it virtually impossible to negate violence altogether from our lives? Doesn't everything involve some form of violence: a mother giving birth to a child or a seed breaking from a pod? Metaphysically speaking, can you discount the presence of creative tension? And isn't all tension violent? How do we then understand violence?

This is a crucial issue. You see, the Jains exemplify this adherence to non-violence. They cover their mouths to prevent germs and other little creatures from going in, some even eschew cloth. But then, going by that, we can't even take medicines to cure ourselves, because we would then be destroying some bacteria at the very least. Buddhism believes in the middle path. In Theravada Buddhism (to differentiate from Mahayana Buddhism), Buddhagosha, the great commentator from Sri Lanka, states clearly, that only monks and nuns could come even close to a non-violent lifestyle. Most lay people, in one way or other, will be violent. We have to be aware of that. My good friend from America, Alan Watts, said that the reason for his being a vegetarian was because cows cry louder than cabbages. So all we can do is to avoid violence as much as possible. The Tibetan Buddhists are not even vegetarians as there is very little vegetation in Tibet. Thai people eat fish. You see, in Siam, the very word for food is *khao pla*—rice and fish. Once you know that you have to commit violence, at least you know how to be less violent. But if you are not careful, you could also *claim* that you avoid violence. There is a difference between avoiding violence and being less violent. We don't kill but we let other people kill for us. We allow capital punishment, we allow conscriptions to the army and we allow nation states to spend so much money on arms. Can we absolve ourselves of responsibility?

Are you vegetarian?

No, I'm not, but if I have a choice, I would prefer to be a non-meat eater.

So, what you are saying is that there ought to be no blanket statement in favour of vegetarianism; it depends on ecology, climatic conditions, local resources, customs, among other things.

The strength and weakness of Buddhism is that it has no rigid dogma. It depends entirely on how one knows oneself. The less one exploits oneself, the less one exploits others. If one is aware, one knows what to do. So 'mindfulness' is the key word in Buddhism.

*In your book, **Seeds of Peace** you write, 'Pacifism is at once a great* strength as well as a great weakness of Buddhism as an organized religion'. Why is it a weakness? Does that mean you would like Buddhism to endorse a holy war, a just war, so long as it is mindfully conducted? I don't think any school of Buddhism subscribes to the 'just war' theory. Violence is violence. In the eyes of the Buddha it is all unskillful. At least, in my tradition, the Pali tradition, the southern school of Buddhism, it is never wise to be violent. But in the northern school of Buddhism, there is one text that was written much later. It had the following example: if I travel in a boat with you, and I know that you are a robber who is going to kill the rest of the passengers, then out of my compassion, I am allowed to kill you. Even so, I commit an act of violence, but in view of the fact that I might be saving the remaining five hundred passengers, perhaps it is my skillful means to kill you. But in the southern school, there is not even a single text to justify violence.

But is human nature not a constant? Haven't we always been violent or tended to be so? Is man today any more violent than his predecessors, though we get the feeling that the pace and quality of modern violence is different from that of a more simple society. Can you comment on this?

If human nature contains the components of violence, it also contains the components of non-violence. Violence in a very simple society probably comprises at most, the use of a stone, a stick or knife. Darwin has been misrepresented, especially in the way that it was put by Spencer—survival of the strongest. Hence competition. I don't think that's right. Competition means that one exploits oneself to begin with. When one works only to compete, one doesn't think properly. Something happens to one's inside and one loses harmony within and without.

I was talking the other day to some students at Jawaharlal Nehru University in New Delhi, and they said competition is the law, violence is the norm. But I say, collaboration is also the norm, non-violence is also the norm. This has to be stressed. Violence has certainly increased today because firstly, the mainstream media thrives on the transportation of violence. Not surprisingly, the best profits are made from arms deals. The connection is clear, once people are sold on violence; that it is easy to push arms. Furthermore, take a look at advertisements which engulf you in a world of hallucinations.

As regards violence, there are some who promote it on a large scale—people like Huntington, who, though old, are still taken seriously. He was the one who advised the American president to bomb all the villages of South Vietnam. So that the Viet-Cong would be driven into the city.

At that time the communists were the enemy; now its the Arabs. Once the 'enemy' idea takes root, violence is bound to increase. So departments of Military Affairs are created, and today this is considered a very respectable field! So one sees how the myth has been gradually created. People need to be aware of this so that they know how to confront it. For instance, we recently had a big gathering in my country to attend a meeting called *Alternatives to Consumerism* to address this whole issue of advertisements.

I gather from what you say that technology and the market system are insecure and want humanity to be violent, weak and exploitative in order for the market to survive?

Precisely. The market can be useful and harmful, but technology is usually harmful. The more complicated technology becomes, the more harmful it is, because one can't comprehend it. Indeed, even our professions—the more complicated they are, the more harmful they become to us. That is why a lot of people spend their time fighting within big corporations and bureaucracies, because it has no meaning. From the Buddhist point of view, there is what is called Right Livelihood, i.e., one must understand what one is doing. All of the stuff we do has no meaning, it is all so compartmentalized.

Do you subscribe to the view that there is a larger-than-life natural cycle at work? That everything goes full circle, plays itself out and balances itself? That we do not have to worry about micro-procedures and trends of nature, proliferating violence or technology? Does this view ever color your activism?

Now, this kind of view could be useful or harmful. If one just sits and waits for violence to decrease, I don't think it will. The Buddha said that if one puts fuel to the fire, the fire will only increase. The point is, that any kind of destruction that one sees in one's lifetime must be challenged, but challenged meaningfully and that means non-violently.

Right now, in my country, there is a big gas pipeline coming from Burma. At first, we all thought, how wonderful, we'll get cheap gas, there's going to be a big industry. People were going to get rich. But when one gives them the facts, one can see who is really going to get rich—the transnational corporations at the expense of the Burmese people who have been maimed, raped, delocated and killed. Is this not violence in the name of technological advancement? If one cuts trees, they don't grow back in a few years. It takes at least a few decades.

One has to bring in awareness, non-violently, and then one can change things. Fritz Schumacher was sent to Burma by the British government when Burma had just become independent around the same time as India, to help them 'develop'. But Fritz was probably the only expert who said that they don't need to develop *our* way, it should be the other way round.

Let me recount an instance that took place when U Nu was the Prime Minister of Burma. Some experts reported that Burma was very rich in uranium and that if it were exploited, she would be the richest country in the world. U Nu asked the expert, 'How long did it take the uranium to form'? 'Millions of years', said the experts. U Nu remarked, 'Oh, then let it remain for a few thousand years more'. Now that is a non-violent approach. Violence is linked with greed and greed is linked to delusion. The five main Buddhist precepts are all indirectly or directly linked to violence anger, greed, sexual misconduct, lies and intoxication. The ideas of the Vietnamese monk, Thich Nhat Hanh have been published in a beautiful book on the five precepts called, **For the Future to be Possible**. Most Buddhists, whom I call capital 'B' Buddhists, deal with the five precepts in a very old fashioned way. It is not enough just to declare yourself free of these; it is too simplistic—the whole social structure is full of violence.

Isn't ideology violent too, I mean the violence of 'ism'?

Yes, most certainly. Any 'ism' for that matter, including Buddhism. The Buddha never used the word 'Buddhism'. It was coined in England. Once one holds the view that my 'ism' is better than yours, one is no longer natural. Any religion has two sides, one tribal and the other universal. Buddhism has a warring side to it too. That's why I sometimes talk about small 'b' buddhism—the buddha-dharma, because the teachings of the Buddha encourage you not to believe, but to listen, study and practice. If you blindly accept the five precepts, you are bound to go astray. It is a goody goody approach.

Are the young people of Siam familiar with Gandhi? Are they curious about him?

I would say more now, because of the efforts of Mr. Karuna Kusalasaya and his wife. He walked all the way from Siam in the 1930s, met Gandhiji and was deeply inspired by him. You see, for all of us, the Buddha is so far away, Gandhi is so much closer. Maha Ghosananda is known as the Gandhi of Cambodia, and Thich Nhat Hanh as the same in Vietnam, though he is a Buddhist monk. Buddhist monks are traditionally good at social improvement at the village level, but they are not very politically aware, and this is where Gandhi's contribution is very important to us. I mean, one must understand politics, but not be involved in party politics. One must challenge politics which includes the international economic order.

Do you ever use fasting as a protest tool? What do you think of fasting? The end may be non-violent, but would you say that the means may be violent?

I don't use fasting for political ends, but I help people who fast. I fast regularly though, during our Buddhist lent. But for me that is training, just like I use training to control, say, my anger. I also use fasting to impress the group of people I work with, that at least we have the *luxury* of fasting. Half the people in the world have to go without food. Naturally, when I fast, there is some violence, but that violence is gentle. When one fasts all the time it becomes natural, it can even be healthy.

Talking of health, what do you make of modern medicine and systems of health? Do you reckon that it could have genetic and generational implications of violence?

Let's face it—when we say 'modern medicine', we mean 'western medicine', which is unfortunately in the hands of a few rich drug companies whose sole motive is profit. Therefore, they are very powerful and almost have the entire medical profession under their control. In Siam, they use all kinds of tactics to perpetuate this; they give free samples, promote and support seminars; etc. I was asked to be one of the judges of the People's Tribunal on the tenth anniversary of Bhopal. We passed judgment in the British Parliament that the present western hospitals and medicine were violent and harmful. If it served anybody, it only served the rich. On top of that, you now have medical technology which is prohibitively expensive. Do you not call it a violence on health? Why have we forsaken Chinese, Thai and Indian systems of medicine on which people have survived for thousands of years? And why do we want to be immortal and prolong death?

You have been travelling all over the world and observing people. Because of global homogenizing processes, the problems and issues faced by young people are also homogenized. What is your message to the youth of India?
Mainstream educational institutions incorporate what I call a 'hidden curriculum' that denigrates the family and the community and which say that indigenous cultures are old fashioned. Therefore, they need to have *alternative* information to empower themselves in a balanced way. Lastly, young middle-class students should spend some time working with the poor, who are more in touch with reality.

[from *The Eye : a written word movement* 71 Vol 5 No 1 Oct.-Dec. 1997, New Delhi.]

A BUDDHIST RESPONSE TO
STRUCTURAL VIOLENCE
AND CONSUMERISM

Sulak Sivaraksa, Thai activist and social critic is a champion of socially engaged Buddhism. The Nobel Prize nominee spoke to *Dharma Life* about the by-products of our consumer culture and outlined alternative ways of living.

Dharma Life: *You have commented that traditional Buddhism has been weak in addressing social issues and have campaigned to change this. Do you see signs of progress?*
Sulak Sivaraksa: It is beginning to change but not significantly. Traditional South-East Asian Buddhism has been good at teaching how to be ethical and generous. People brought up in Asian Buddhist cultures were often very generous. This was partly due to living in an agrarian society, which helps people to relate with each other, with nature and with animals.

Once generosity was built into the culture, people felt it was good when a bird took some of their rice or a squirrel took fruit from a tree. Buddhist ethics helped to build a culture in which violence was not admired, stealing was discouraged, and generosity was emphasized. The culture did not promote lust and on the whole people were fairly truthful. Until recently very few people took intoxicants.

This changed in the last century because we wanted to imitate the West. Industrialization is the norm in the West, which emphasizes the rights of the middle classes and capitalism. This has led to consumerism. As our society linked with the outside world, it became part of an international economic order and, in turn, this brought structural violence into society. Political corruption followed, as politicians became crooked and began to use false speech and to buy votes. This has been the pattern in Siam for the past 40 years. In Siam Buddhism has not been very successful in tackling these issues because the practice of generosity is itself open to corruption. In the old days people gave money to build a temple because it would be useful as an educational and cultural centre, as well as for their own peace of mind. Now people build temples because they want to be socially recognized.

This description of popular Buddhist practice, however, only includes the first two steps in Buddhist training: generosity and ethics. We now need to emphasize the third step: mindfulness. Generosity is ultimately about giving up selfhood, but you can't stop being selfish unless you have a critical self-awareness, and the key to that is mindfulness. With mindfulness you know how to avoid harming yourself at a subtle level. Then you will love yourself in the most positive sense of the term and therefore come to love others, rather than exploit them.

What do you mean when you speak of the structural violence in society?

People in industrial society avoid being obviously unethical in their personal lives, particularly in a Buddhist country like Siam. But they fail to realize that their livelihood is itself a form of stealing. It is structural violence for the rich to live a luxurious, wasteful lifestyle that destroys natural resources, which makes the gap between rich and poor greater and greater. Many people are slowly starving, while others are eating too much. Most people in Siam practice Buddhist precepts only in a general way and don't realize how they are implicated in an unethical system. Advertisements, for example, promote greed—so in a sense they indirectly promote stealing—let alone the fact that they may use false speech, or promote drugs, alcohol and cigarettes.

Most people who practise traditional Buddhism don't realize the contradiction. Even meditators may develop inner calm yet lack a broader social awareness. In Burma there are wonderful meditation masters, but they have tolerated a dictatorship since 1962. If Buddhists have a lack of social awareness, which isn't informed through meditation, they can be full of violence, such as some monks in Sri Lanka who support militarism.

Understanding the structural violence in society inevitably involves politics. There are so many important questions that are themselves political. How important is the army? I think spending the national budget on arms instead of health or education is stealing. Likewise, is modern banking lending? Is all this money lending not stealing? What about the World Bank? Since we started the International Network of Engaged Buddhists (INEB) 10 years ago, we have been talking about these issues. Before that many Japanese Buddhists didn't realize there was anything wrong with Japan exploiting the rest of Asia. Now a number of Japanese Buddhists are concerned to do something for social justice.

Is there a precedent for this extension of Buddha's teaching?

Last year when I met the Dalai Lama I asked: 'You are a wonderful example of cultivating love for the enemy and it's great to have compassion and understanding, but what about the structural violence in society?' He told me he had no idea. But he was wonderful—so simple and honest, saying: 'We're here to learn'. So Buddhism may not have developed all the answers to our modern situation. We must learn not only from Buddhism but also from other religions. That's why I have invited many leading Muslims, Christian, Hindus and Jews, who are concerned with resolving social conflicts, to the forthcoming Alternatives to Consumerism Conference.

The title "Alternatives to Consumerism" implies a positive way forward. What are those alternatives?

The main characteristics of the alternative approach are: firstly, self-reliance, so that people find the resources in their own communities that enable them to resist consumerism. Secondly, there must be a raised awareness. Many successful projects in Siam, where a community has escaped from poverty under the guidance of Buddhism, are now threatened because consumerism has crept in by way of the new pulpit—television. Thirdly, people must be empowered spiritually, and be proud of their local culture. Consumerism exerts pressure towards forming a monoculture. Furthermore, fundamentalist strands of religion that rigidly dictate how one should live also tend to create monoculture. We need to promote cultural diversity, which implies promoting the democratic process. These are the main characteristics of alternatives to consumerism.

Why do you emphasize that consumerism is a particularly pernicious problem, which is central to how our societies are organized?

Consumerism is the personification of greed and people don't realise that one can die for greed just as one can die for nationalism. It drives a person to work too hard, to desire money and to consume. One is conditioned to think that without consumer goods one is nobody. 'I buy therefore I am' is the slogan of the modern age. We must understand consumerism as a new demonic religion and find a spiritual alternative.

This is where the communists failed. They only empowered people through ideology, just like the Church in the Middle Ages. If one didn't accept the ideology of the Church, one was condemned. The communists were the same. If one didn't buy Mao Tse Tung's thought, or follow Marx and Lenin, one was a revisionist.

We don't need more ideology—even Buddhist ideology. We need the spirit. We don't want to make people Buddhist with a capital B, but to offer ways that people can naturally share together. The spirit is the strongest thing about a human being and it's one thing consumerism doesn't have. It has everything else: money, power, the best brains, the media under its control. But if we go to the essence of religious teaching, we can find something that offers a real alternative to consumerism.

We may not destroy consumerism but we will surely build an alternative. There are a number of communities doing this, both in the north and the south. I believe consumerism will destroy itself because, as George Orwell said of the Soviet Union, any system without moral legitimacy will destroy itself. Sixty years ago the Soviet Union was considered an alternative to capitalism but it had no moral legitimacy, that's why it collapsed. Even if consumerism is not destroyed as soon as we'd like, we can at least create an alternative—so that when it dies something beautiful will be reborn.

Most of our lives are deeply enmeshed in a consumer society, making it difficult for people to imagine how to disentangle themselves. How can we disentangle ourselves from consumerism without withdrawing from the world?

The basis of the Buddhist view of life is expressed in the first of the Four Noble Truths—that all life includes suffering. Consumerism hopes to avoid suffering, but Buddhism would say this is turning away from the truth. We might think: 'Maybe a

car is better than our legs, a bigger house better than simple living'.
In this way we become attracted to buying. The consequence is
ignorance: the rich don't realize their lifestyle depends on depriving
the poor. So, we must confront suffering.

The legend of Prince Siddhartha demonstrates this. He left
his palace and saw the poor, the dead, the aged, the sick, and
that motivated him to seek the truth. Most people in the world
suffer tremendously and one must be exposed to it. We must learn
from the poor and share with them. Of course rich people also
suffer, but consumerism offers them a way to avoid experiencing
their suffering. So Buddhists should not just rely on meditation.
Meditation helps, but you must also confront worldly suffering. That's
the first step in disentangling ourselves.

*According to the Worldwatch Institute more goods and services were
consumed by people between 1950 and 1990 than by all previous
generations. Do you hold out any hope for slowing the runaway train
of consumerism?*

Perhaps these figures are misleading. The top 10 percent
consumes far more than anyone a few generations ago. Yet the
great majority consumes less in comparison with their predecessors.
Most people one-hundred years ago at least had access to simple
food, lodging and medicine.

Also previous generations were not brainwashed by notions
of 'development' to feel inferior or underdeveloped. Many people
are gradually empowering themselves and seeking an alternative.
I have hope that through being empowered spiritually, confronting
suffering mindfully, and understanding the causes of suffering in
consumerism, we will be able to overcome it.

What is happening at the Alternatives to Consumerism Conference?

Throughout December there will be a series of seminars and
workshops in Siam. The main event will be the Inter-religious
Spirituality and Consumerism Seminar. I want people to make friends
and enjoy themselves in a spiritual and cultural atmosphere. There
will be song, dance and celebrations, so we will use our heads
and hearts together. Then hopefully we can draw up something
common to agree upon, and we will work together on that over
the next three to five years.

I hope our gathering will help us to find alternatives to

the negative approaches to religion that foster consumerism. In Siam we have the Dharmakaya, which wants to use 1,000 kgs of gold to make a statue of their founder. Similarly the Pope wants to build huge cathedrals in Africa, where people have no food. This is why we want to bring spiritual leaders together to emphasize that religion is not about material aggrandizement. We need to return to spirit. Christianity needs to return to the spirit of Saint Francis of Assisi. Buddhists should bring the message of the Buddha home. This has always been the aim of my work: to understand Buddhist teachings in their proper sense and apply them in the complicated system of the modern world.

[from *Dharma Life : Buddhism for Today*, Winter 1997, Cambridge, England.]

STRUCTURAL VIOLENCE
AND SPIRITUALITY

Socially Engaged Buddhist Perspectives

Donald Rothberg: In a talk at the conference "Toward a Dhammic Society," held in Thailand in February 1995, you maintained that an understanding of structural violence is at the core of engaged Buddhism.

Sulak Sivaraksa: Before talking about structural violence, let me give some background about Buddhism and traditional Buddhist societies in Southeast Asia. Buddhism teaches the elimination of violence entirely, both intrapsychically and interpersonally. Violence is connected with what Buddhists call the "Three Poisons": greed, hatred, and delusion. Transforming those poisons occurs in the context of the *sangha* (the spiritual community), which was set up to eliminate violence. Members of monastic communities, for example, attempt to live a harmonious life with the other monks and nuns, lay people, animals and the environment. Even lay people avoid professions that are linked to violence, such as trading in arms, intoxicants, slaves, animals, or being a soldier. Lay people also practice the Five Ethical Precepts (refraining from killing, stealing, harmful speech, sexual misconduct, and misuse of drugs) and try to avoid violence as much as possible.

In simple agrarian societies, the issue of structural violence arises infrequently, although hierarchies according to wealth, power and gender exist. For example, my wife's grandmother is regarded as a very rich lady in her province in Siam, but her lifestyle is almost exactly the same as everyone around her. Her mother had to tend the fields just like any of the poorer people. With the wealth she accumulated, she built a traditional temple to help develop the *sangha.*

The weakness of Buddhism in Southeast Asia is that Buddhists do not deal with the power structure which, even in Buddhist kingdoms, has always been guided by Hindu values. That arrangement is based on the theory of the chariot that needs "two wheels": the wheel of righteousness is represented by the monastic *sangha*, the wheel of power by the king.

Monks would talk to the rulers, but refrained from holding power. They gave consolation to soldiers and went on military expeditions, although the Buddha limited such trips by the monks to one week. The Buddha generally saw the state as being like a poisonous snake. One does not kill it; that would be violence. One deals with it through "skillful means"—being kind, but remembering that it is a poisonous snake! Unfortunately, in the last one-hundred years this critical view of the state has not been stressed in Siam.

The weakness in the separation of the "two wheels" is that a person who avoids power does not understand much about it. The *sangha* tries to influence the state to be less violent. But at least in the Southern school of Buddhism, the attempt to eliminate violence is entirely on the *personal* level, occurring ideally through the career of the monk or nun. This demonstrates a minimal understanding of structural violence.

In the last fifty years, the Western model of "development" has largely transformed the traditional rural way of life, which was centered in the village and temple; as a result structural violence has greatly increased. In this period, Buddhist alternatives to development have been largely limited to small communities of forest monks who avoid and ignore the values and violence of main-stream society. That approach presupposes that violence does not reach the forest, that the forest will be protected. But who nowadays can protect the forest? In the old days, the righteous ruler had to protect the animals and the forest as well as the villages.

Nowadays, violence, spread by the greed of capitalism and empire, has become the norm; there is nowhere to go. Even many Buddhists accept this norm. The present Secretary-General of the National Economic Development Board that runs Siam is a practicing Buddhist! He is a very nice man and close to the king; he may meditate and act generously. But he has no choice but to go along with the international economic order; he must accept capitalism and structural violence. "Of course," he might say, "it's not ideal, and there is some greed. But it is the norm. We cannot use Buddhism to stop greed or war. War is the normal way of the world. Buddhism never stopped war in the past."

Structural Violence, Ethics, and Power

DR: In using the term "structural violence," we identify phenomena as violent that are not usually seen as violent. For example, Western economic domination of the world is usually not seen as violent, at least by most Westerners. Buddhists may also not link a response to structural violence with their more personal conception of following the ethical guidelines (sila). They may not consider cutting down the forests, or allowing many women to become prostitutes, or using pesticides to be violations of the ethical precepts.

SS: Again, in the old days of the temple and rural community, questions of structural violence were not so relevant. One could follow the Five Precepts fairly easily. Killing is bad, and the idea of killing is also bad, because hatred arises. Stealing is bad because greed arises. Sexual misconduct is typically rooted in lust; unskillful speech (such as lying) is based in delusion, and so on. But now hatred, greed, lust, and lying pervade our whole culture, through various institutions and the media. We accept them as part of our lives!

I have learned that many Thai monks love to watch a Taiwanese soap opera about the Chief Justice of China in the Sung period, even though this man chops off people's heads every night! The stories teach a Confucian sense of justice, in which it is okay that someone has to be killed. Or we accept it when Mr. Kissinger says, "Two million Cambodians must die in order to save the world." Or when Mr. Truman drops the bomb on Hiroshima and Nagasaki. Of course, we are not among those people in Nagasaki.

DR: Your last examples point to another aspect of structural violence. Some structural violence may be invisible or not seen as violence. But your last examples would be seen as examples of violence that are *acceptable* for the working of the system. That is related to the idea that some people's suffering matters and some people's suffering is acceptable or even does not matter. At the moment in the United States, the violence of street crime, which makes middle-class people fearful, is often seen as unacceptable. It is not acceptable to have the streets be unsafe for some people, but it is acceptable to kill 200,000 Iraqis in the Gulf War!

Santikaro Bhikkhu: I'd like to relate structural violence to our own conceptions of power and human nature and to inner selfishness. I have learned from Theravāda Buddhism as well as from my teacher, Ajahn Buddhadasa, and from meditation that there are two kinds of power. One kind of power is the power of one person or group *over* and *against* another person or group (or the environment). A second kind of power is more akin to "authority." One may have great influence over people, but without force and without going against their wills. For example, many people would be willing to do what my teacher asked, not because he has any direct coercive power over them, but because of his moral or spiritual authority. This is an ideal that lies behind the old Buddhist models of the king, who is supposed to possess the "Ten Virtues." That sometimes is forgotten under the influence of Hindu concepts.

The first kind of coercive power fits well with notions of the state held by Western philosophers such as Hobbes and Locke; human beings are basically selfish and need to be controlled. In the Buddhist ideal, however, human beings are able to develop spiritually, to lessen their selfishness. That latter view leads to a different sense of power or authority, more of a moral one that is grounded in meditative experience. The first kind of power is the power of ego that a despotic ruler (whether a king, a dictator, the directors of multinational corporations, the International Monetary Fund (IMF), U.S. Agency for International Development (AID), or the World Bank) can project into structural violence. Such power controls huge numbers of people without their consent, without even asking them.

If we look deeply into our own urges and habits of using power over others, which we can observe fairly easily, it comes down to a *desire to control*. That desire comes from a sense of a self that wants something from others. Out of that wanting, we project and create self, and that self is an inner tool for control. Buddhist practice has as its aim to move out of this desire for control; it leads to a different model of society, with much less coercion. But viewing human nature as inherently selfish, and in need of coercion to ensure the good, results in another model. Structural violence has its roots in this attempt to control—individually, interpersonally, in groups such as families, and in larger social structures.

DR: The vision of liberal democracy as it developed with Locke and with the architects of the American Revolution is of a society in which individuals, at least in theory, are able to follow their own desires, which purportedly lead to their own happiness. The role of the state is to make possible for people to follow their desires without being oppressed or coerced by the state, by other major institutions, or by each other. But what has happened, presumably from the beginning in the United States, because democracy was very incomplete (most of the population could not vote), is that some individuals, following their desires, have in sometimes complicated ways (often through institutions) prevented others from following their desires. The result often translates into violence and suffering.

SB: What you just said helps point out some of the inherent weaknesses of liberal democracy; whatever its merits, it is primarily designed to give freedom to individual desires. From a Buddhist perspective, that is hopeless. Individual desires are bound to collide with each other; the emphasis should also be on communities, not just on individuals. By taking the individual out of the context of relationships in families, communities, and culture generally, we do not see the whole being.

SS: Of course, many people directing development, whether in Japan or the World Bank, have wonderful intentions. They are not necessarily selfish, unenlightened or power hungry, but their thinking is compartmentalized and thereby serves to legitimize structural violence. For example, they may reflect, "Okay, we have choices A, B, and C, and we'll choose C. It's not ideal, but we have to do it this way. We have to sacrifice one thing in order to do another." Sometimes they are aware of the consequences of their actions; they know that some people will suffer from development policies. These people are not foolish but they say, "Once we become an economy like Taiwan or South Korea, there will be less suffering." However, they don't want *their* daughters to be prostitutes!

DR.: Why is the suffering connected with development not seen as violence? Why is it seen as acceptable?

SS: A basic problem is that development is seen only as having to do with the economic, technological, and social dimensions of life, rather than with moral and spiritual dimensions as well. Most of what we get from the West only treats the externals of life. For example, mainstream Western medicine only deals with the body and not with the mind and spirit.

DR.: Structural violence is commonly linked with a limited conception of human beings, such that we may neglect our ethical, intellectual, and spiritual lives.

SS: Precisely. This is where we must link the question of structural violence to *sila*, to ethics. The roots of structural violence are in the ways in which we are not harmonious with ourselves and each other. As that lack of harmony builds up, it becomes structural violence.

Responding to Structural Violence

DR.: How do people become aware that what we call "structural violence" contains violence just as real as inter-personal violence? It is not particularly a focus of newspapers.

SS: From a Buddhist perspective, the starting point is to *become self-aware*, to become aware of one's own violence. Many activists—for example, the Greens, the socialists, or the communists—may speak out clearly about many forms of "external violence", but they may not be very aware of their own internal violence and how they act with the people around them. For this reason, nonviolence is an important foundation. If one is violent toward one's self and with others, then the violence tends to become more and more structural.

The Buddhist teaching about "dependent origination" (*paticca-samuppāda*), the "inter-being" of all things, is helpful for seeing structural violence. For example, think of the Gulf War in terms of the many different interrelationships. The Gulf War occurred because Americans had to have cheap oil. They did not care how many Iraqis died. Furthermore, getting oil requires big oil companies whose board members are most interested in continued production and high profits. They also need people to continue driving cars. So more roads are needed and there is less public transportation: fewer railroads, fewer bicycles, fewer trees. And where does the oil come from? It comes from the Middle East, so the Middle East must be under U.S. control. If countries are not under American control, they must be enemies of the United States—so Mr. Saddam Hussein is presented as a second Hitler.

DR: So we must have armies, research on military technologies, and large sums set aside in our budgets to help us control the oil. We try to control the Iraqis, to have the right leader, and we don't care what they do to their own people.

SB: There also has to be control over the U.S. population, especially through the large multinational corporations, the government bureaucracies, the education systems, and so on.

SS: All the levels are interrelated. If a person does not know who he or she is, then that person is controlled by greed, hatred, and delusion. We think that we are somehow better than others; we as a nation can guide the world economy better, or police the world more effectively. This is dualistic; we don't see that people on the other side, other races or classes or nations, are just like us, perhaps more clever or more stupid, but most basically just like us, all with the potentiality to become enlightened Buddhas, full of love and wisdom.

DR: Few Buddhists, whether in the United States or apparently in Thailand as well, have much understanding of structural violence; they don't typically apply the teaching of "dependent origination," or other traditional teachings and practices to structural issues. How can seeing one's own violence lead to seeing and acting on structural violence?

SS: Actually, most so-called Buddhists do not even look very deeply into themselves. But if someone has come to understand himself or herself well, the next step is to *confront suffering*, that is, to follow the first of the Buddha's Four Noble Truths. But how do we find the cause of suffering when greed, hatred, and delusion are institutionalized and structural? We have to understand and transform the structures. We have to see how greed is present in consumerism and capitalism; how hatred is linked with centralization, state power, and the military; how delusion is present in our education and media. Then we can change those structures through the Buddha's Noble Eightfold Path. But without personal transformation, social or structural transformation is not possible. This is where Buddhists challenge Marxists. If Buddhists can connect personal and social transformation, then we can make a contribution.

SB: One reason that meditation is not more concerned with structures is a kind of arrogance that can creep into meditative practice. Buddhist meditators may find important insights in their practices, but sometimes they assume that everything else is not important: "Meditation is the only way." A second reason is connected with a more subtle form of arrogance. Often we think that the problems are so big and that we are so small: "What can I do? I have to do something." So we give up, saying, "Well, there's nothing I can do." That is the arrogance of thinking that I can do something alone, a terrible illusion that cripples many Buddhists. So I would add a third step to the two that Sulak mentioned: we need to create truly effective *communities* and *organizations*. But we tend to be very individualistic. Until we look inside, confront suffering internally and externally, and then build groups and communities, we have no chance of dealing with social structures.

It is easy to sit alone in the forest, to be calm. People may go on meditation retreats and be very happy and blissful. They think that they are enlightened, that they have accomplished something. On returning to their families, friends, and jobs, they are dismayed when all the old, bad, painful conflicts return.

When one works with others, one's greed, anger, and delusion surface, because of course other people do something that one likes and some that one dislikes. But the members of a supportive community can share common values and understandings and generally treat each other kindly. Within that context, it is easier to face the defilements that arise when we rub up against each other. It is easier to become aware of our sexist habits, or our partriarchal structures and paternalistic behavior, or our attempts to manipulate and control. Of course, those behaviors will not disappear overnight. Nonetheless, a healthy community can help to connect looking inside—getting to know ourselves—and looking outside at what is going on in society. A community helps us to deal with the social issues on a comprehensible and concrete level. If we can transform behavior on that level, then maybe there is hope for doing it on a larger level.

SS: We must see also the structural violence in ourselves, in our lifestyles and relationships with others. If we do not confront those issues in our own communities and with our friends, then we compromise our commitment to ending structural violence. Of course, we can speak humbly and positively so that our criticisms are not harmful, but friendship must also have a critical dimension at times. The Buddha said that friends become our "other voice."

Questioning Development and the Global Economy

SS: I am also hopeful about transforming structural violence in the world because such violence, particularly the violence of development, has recently become less and less legitimate from an ethical perspective. People increasingly see through the lies of the IMF and the big banks, through justifications of gender inequality, and so on.

SB: One questionable aspect of "development" is its paternalistic nature. Development on the global as well as national levels has been something that one group does to another. It is top-down and inherently violent when decisions are made in Washington or New York or Rome, then conveyed to Bangkok or Kuala Lampur, then spread out through the various bureaucracies. In some cases, the local culture supports the paternalism. For example, many people in Southeast Asia have grown up with paternalism. In Thailand, it is okay for the elder brother and one's teachers to make decisions about one's life.

People now are realizing the extent to which paternalism is a cover, in terms of development, for one group controlling and taking advantage of another. The farmers in Thailand are starting to wake up to the government rhetoric about development, which is supposed to bring them a better standard of living. But this is not happening. The price of rice is still not enough for farmers to make a profit.

DR: I wonder how a vigorous questioning of the goals of development in the West can help to de-legitimize such goals. Enrique Dussel, a prominent liberation theologian living in Mexico City, once told me that he thought it crucial for people in the United States to develop their own liberation theology and practice. He thought that an undermining from within, as it were, of the prevailing model of middle-class life and capitalist development could be very helpful.

SS: Of course, if middle-class Americans could change, it would help the world. But in our country, I think what we need is bottom-up development, which is now taking place. An increasing number of voices are saying, "No. The model of development from the government is violent and rooted in greed, hatred, and delusion. We want to use the Buddha's approach of self-sufficiency, self-sustainability, and at the same time personal development, community development, and development with ecological balance." Of course, we can link our movement with similar movements in the West.

SB: It would be wonderful if people in the United States were to develop their own liberation theology, but the rest of the world would be stupid to wait. Considering the high standard of consumer living to which many Americans are addicted and their lack of a sense of alternatives, how much capacity have Americans to change or to think for themselves?

In places like Thailand, the majority of the population can still remember a rural existence in which power was not used in such blatant, ugly ways. In Bangkok, you can see everything that is wrong with advanced capitalism in the United States. But still, many people in Bangkok have grandparents or aunts and uncles in the provinces who remember another way of life. In the West, for most of us, that is three generations back.

SS: In the 1950s, when the idea of development spread over the world, an American expert came to this country and said that Buddhism was the main barrier to development. He said that the Buddha teaches people to be content. If one is content, then a poor man is as good as the richest man. The American said, "That is dangerous!" The government accepted the views of the American expert and asked the senior members of the monkhood to tell monks not to teach on that issue! They put notices up everywhere in the late 1950s saying, "Work is money. Money is Work. Both produce happiness." It had a tremendous effect. For thirty years now, people have believed that one works only for money, whether it is honest or dishonest work, legal or illegal. Now we are paying the price of such views.

We have imitated the West so dreadfully for the last thirty or forty years that our consciousness of the negative aspects of development have been quickened. Bangkok has become a horrible place only in the last thirty years.

The General Agreement on Tariffs and Trade (GATT) reflects, I believe, a new and dangerous form of structural violence, promoting greed at the international level and at the expense of the communities and nations. Someone like me, running bookshops and small publishing houses, may within five or ten years be out of a job, because the Japanese will likely come in a big way, even publishing in Thai through their computers. GATT is designed to help the most advanced and efficient sectors of the international economy—a crowning achievement of structural violence.

I will give an example. I was running a bookshop in Bangkok. The owners of the building where I worked threw us out and are now building a 20-story high technology center—in the name of development. They also threw out the nearby dentists, the noodle-sellers, the poor people who came to sell things and the middle-class people who came to buy things. It was a wonderful community. We were helping each other. But now, in the name of development and efficiency, the community has been dispersed.

SB: I disagree with Sulak that GATT is a *new* form of violence. When I hear about GATT, I first think about the opium war when, in the name of free trade, the British forced the Chinese to accept British opium from India. Similarly, a few years ago, in the name of free trade, the American government put a lot of pressure on Thailand to accept American tobacco. Before then, people smoked Thai tobacco. A lot of farmers in the areas where I used to live grew their own tobacco; there was also very little advertising. Once the big American tobacco companies came in, there was tobacco advertising all over the place. These are just two examples of how, in the name of free trade, something very immoral took place. To me, GATT is not *free* trade. What is called "free trade" means that people with the military, political, and economic power can sell what they want, wherever they want. It is free just for them, not for the rest.

Individualism and Resistance to Addressing Structural Issues

SB: The recent growth of interest in spirituality in the West does not necessarily involve challenging the deeper social structures. For example, all the people who are battered and beaten by the middle-class lifestyle can go off and do a meditation retreat once a year or go to a national park so that they can heal themselves a bit and go back to work. But such spirituality supports the system, unless it poses moral questions about the system. In a simpler society, it may have been possible for a spiritually oriented person to distance herself or himself and not participate in structural violence. I do not think it is possible now. As Sulak said, the forests are getting mowed down. We may try to help someone through spiritual practices, but the person just goes home and is caught in the same meat grinder.

DR: Some temples in northeast Thailand are in fact supported by money from prostitution.

SS: If Buddhists are going to contribute anything to the modern world, we must state clearly that violence is inherent in all established societies. That is what it means to confront suffering (Buddhism's First Noble Truth). To examine the causes of suffering (the Second Noble Truth), one cannot talk in the abstract. Consumerism, materialism, and development policies have to be spelled out.

DR: Many people in the West and, increasingly, in Thailand would say, "I do my job. I try to make enough money to live on. I have enough problems with my personal situation. Now you tell me I have to look at these social issues, these ecological issues, these enormous issues. I do not want to listen to you!"

SS: But if they do not want to listen to me, then they are

also part of the problem, part and parcel of the structural violence in the system.

SB: We have to find ways to meet people in their own day-to-day lives and communicate with them effectively. Over and over again, those of us who raise issues about structural violence in Thailand are criticized as being aggressive or violent in our speech even if we use very polite words and do not accuse anybody. But although some self-interest may be involved in not wanting to look at structural violence, there are also deep myths that people were raised with, myths of how wonderful Buddhism is, of how wonderful our country is, or of how good and innocent we are. To let go of those myths is very difficult; to help people see through such myths is one main way to begin to address structural violence.

Note

This conversation took place in Bangkok, Thailand, in March 1995.

Sulak Sivaraksa of Bangkok, Thailand, is probably that country's most prominent social critic and activist and a major contemporary proponent of socially engaged Buddhism. He has founded rural development projects and many nongovernmental organizations dedicated to exploring alternative models of development. He is the co-founder of the International Network of Engaged Buddhists and the author of many books, including *Religion and Development* (1986), *A Socially Engaged Buddhism* (1998), and *Seeds of Peace* (1992). He has been twice nominated for the Nobel Peace Prize and in 1995 received the Right Livelihood Award.

Santikaro Bhikkhu is an American who has been an ordained monk in Thailand for twelve years. He studied at the Suan Mokkhabalarama ("Garden of Liberation") monastery under the late Buddhadasa Bhikkhu, translating his talks and assisting with retreats. He has been active in many social development workshops in Thailand, the Philippines, India, Nepal, and the United States and is the co-editor of *Entering the Realm of Reality: Towards Dhammic Societies* (1997).

Donald Rothberg is on the faculty of the Saybrook Institute in San Francisco. He has taught and written on socially engaged spirituality, critical social theory, transpersonal studies, and epistemology and mysticism, and is the co-editor of the forthcoming *Ken Wilber in Dialogue: Conversations with Leading Transpersonal Thinkers* (1998). He has served on the board of the Buddhist Peace Fellowship and has helped to guide its BASE (Buddhist Alliance for Social Engagement) training program, developing a spiritual and group form for those working in social service and social action.

[from *ReVision* Vol 20 No 2 USA.]

A BUDDHIST PERSPECTIVE OF RE-ENVISIONING "DEVELOPMENT"

The following draft attempts to re-evaluate the process of "modern development" from a Buddhist perspective. As such, it draws largely from the "development" process within Asia while incorporating insights into the recent Asian financial crisis. The paper, however, is also intended to internally re-envision development as it concerns the way all societies in the world have been pursuing "development". It consists of three parts: a critique of "modern development", a Buddhist vision, and propositions for present engagament. While the critique may at times be rather acerbic, the intention of this paper is to broaden dialogue between disparate groups in the "development" process and to avoid pigeon-holing those perceived "at fault".

I. The Crisis of "Development"

A) Incompleteness of the Modern Development Model

In re-evaluating the role of "devolopment" for the 21st century, we need to make a fundamental re-assessment of the values and methods of envisioning human and social development which have evolved during the last 200 years. From perspectives that grew and stand outside of the modernist approach, such as Buddhism, a critical limitation appears: the over-reliance on quantitative and structural frameworks, most notably in the domination of economic models for engineering human and social well-being. This reliance is characteristic of the preponderance of development agency-staffs of economists and other "experts" trained in the modern social "sciences." It is further manifested in the prevalent use of quantitative evaluation of human and social well-being, such as infant mortality rates, life expectancy rates, literacy rates, consumption rates, poverty rates etc. From a Buddhist perspective, such fragmentation and abstraction belittles the immense diversity and complexity of the human condition.

The underpinnings of such a framework presuppose the ideas of capital markets, nation state structures, the "free individual" (i.e. consumer), and the linear and unlimited process of growth. These are the foundations of a world-view for the vast majority of the West, large segments of Japan, and increasing numbers of southern elites who study abroad. However, for the larger percentage of humanity, these values are alien. Barter and community economies still predominate. Feudal patronage systems are the common political means. The individual is subsumed within roles of duty and obligation. Growth is a cyclical movement of indulgence and renunciation.

In the past fifty years of modernity we have seen the clash of these ill-fitting world-views. Although the modern structural approach has brought great promise in material prosperity, democratic government, and individual social mobility, the preponderance of a purely structural approach has been self-defeating. This top down mechanism for enacting the abstract and structural upon the real and diverse has empowered still feudal state structures to extend their power over their citizens. Further, the belittlement and replacement of indigenous values and systems by these "scientific" and modern structures has complemented this process of disempowerment for the larger mass of citizens.

What is taking place today in the "developing" world is not the modern ideal of the free individual enjoying material prosperity amidst democratic government, but a tragic warping of this vision: material prosperity exists for a small group of government and business elite; feudal cronyism is disguised as representative democracy; and a mass of disempowered citizens are increasingly cut-off from their historical identities. These identities are replaced with modern consumer identities which have few personal or communal resources for coming to grips with.

A typical example of this process comes from the "development" of the Lake Songkla region in Southern Siam. This rural, agricultural based culture and the values that are inseparable from it continue to lose ground to the urban consumer pseudo-culture and all that it breeds. This trend is exemplified by the automated harvester combines. It is extremely rare to find anyone in this region who does not hire a combine to harvest rice. Although it is quicker than harvesting by hand, what is lost are the many rich traditions and customs which provided the bond of village life as each family was dependent on the others for their help in harvesting rice. The songs, dances, communal meals, cooperation, and sense of the whole village being one's home is vanishing. Instead there is a quick swap of money to the stranger from up north who rents out the combine, this grinding, mechanical monster which lumbers over the land. It leaves feeling of competitiveness, isolation and separateness in its wake.

Most villages are no longer self-sufficient and naturally cooperative. For one thing, most working-age people go into factories around Songkhla and Had Yai each day, leaving only the very young and old in the villages. In many cases, whole families or villages have immigrated permanently to the urban areas for low paying jobs and often wind up living in the most unhealthy, dangerous places. We stopped in Songkhla and talked with the residents from one of the ten major slum areas—quaint, quiet little Songkhla is packed with slums! They have organized themselves to call on the government to provide various services (services which they used to take care of by themselves) and to provide support for each other).

B) The Moral Rot Within Structures

The result of such "development" has led to an incredible deterioration of moral and cultural values. The predominance of the modern structural development model, especially economics, has meant a growing breakdown of human values in developing countries. The Asian economic crisis has highlighted this corruption in the government sector as present feudalistic leaders (Thai politicians, the Suharto family) have fused modern market values with elitist patronage in embezzling large amounts of development aid for themselves and seeing that the aid that is implemented is used for their personal business interests. This has had a cascading effect on the societies at large. Sectors of society, especially government officials, seek to get their own slice of the pie at the expense of the public welfare.

When our monastery recently upgraded its quarterly journal (the longest continuously running Buddhist periodical in Siam), our publisher offered it to schools along with other Buddhist books they carry. The librarians in many of these government schools demanded a "commission," 10 percent of the sale to go into their own pockets. Everyone knows that the generals take their multi-million baht commissions from big weapons and plane purchases (as well as government officials from development aid allocations). Are we to be shocked when ordinary teachers also want a cut from religious books?

On the citizen level, this breakdown of cultural values and replacement by market values has led to a gross and unbounded consumerism on display in largely unlivable cities like Bangkok, Jakarta and Manila. With economists calling for greater consumer demand to create domestic growth, urban citizens displaced from their cultural roots in the countryside embrace consumption as a new means of identity. Results have had intolerable environmental effects, from industrial waste and consumer pollution to an explosion of HIV/AIDS in booming sex industries. Crime, religious funda-mentalism and violence (e.g. Indonesia) have also been responses that reassert the identity of those increasingly alienated in the development process.

C) The Role of Development Agencies

The essential difficulty in this "development" process appears to be that structural reform has come before the development of human capacity to deal with it. World Bank President James Wolfensohn on his recent visit to Siam said, "We have the strong belief that people in this country don't want charity. They want to hope, work and do, it themselves". However, recent Bank initiatives in "community development" to meet the Thai crisis with irrigation projects and supporting development in food processing still disregard the need for individuals to make sense of the development process on their own terms.

The World Bank and IMF have properly attacked government corruption in "developing" countries, but they have yet to address the more fundamental dissonance with modern stuctural models and indigenous cultural systems. The moral and cultural corruption undercutting the "development" process will actually only increase with the IMF's "structural re-adjustment" packages. Dismantling government patronage systems (however flawed) and the unbridled plunging of the world market and global consumerism will strip away any lingering vestiges of indigenous frameworks by which "developing" countries make sense of their world. Some see such "structural re-adjustment" as the freeing up of markets. Others might view it as a cultural "clear cut". Expecting foreign multi-nationals to have more concern than feudal bosses have for their own people is a flawed perception brought to light by the tarnished record of northern corporations in the "developing" world (e.g. Nike in Indonesia and Vietnam, Union Carbide in India).

As the developing world is being constantly reminded to reevaluate its operating systems towards greater structural openness and freedom in markets and government, so too must development agencies reevaluate their openness to new ways of envisioning the development process. These agencies need to expand their perspectives for interacting with donor groups. Policy planning and evaluation based on purely quantitative analysis (e.g. GNP, doctors/square kilometer, etc.) does not address the full range of human concerns which create prosperity and happiness. Nor does it resolve, but rather enhances the power hierarchies in these societies. Furthermore, in the process of such a perspective change, there will be a need to develop a common language between donor agencies and their recipients which gives account to human and social diversity and respects cultural identities.

II. Buddhism—An Inside-Out Approach to Development
A) "Human Resource Development" as Personal Transformation

As an indigenous tradition with over two and a half millennia of application, Buddhism offers a complimentary perspective on human and social "development". In the early development years of post World War II Asia, Buddhism was stereotypically viewed as an anathema to "modern development". While Buddhism does indeed have reservations about the course of "modern development", its finely tuned practices of inner-cultivation as well as the recent emergence of "development monks" in countries like Siam, belie the notion that Buddhism is complacent either about individual or social transformation.

These finely tuned practices of inner transformation offer important resources in developing the capacity of individuals transforming society. They also present a culturally appropriate model for "human resource development" in Asia as opposed to the present model of education for industrial labor and consumption. Buddhism has balanced the need for structural models to envision and guide growth and development as well as the need for the unfolding of diverse and unique characteristics in each situation. The Theravada school which predominates in Southeast Asia along with the Tibetan schools emphasize more a structural approach, while the Mahayana schools of East Asia such as Zen and Pure Land espouse more free form practices. In either stream, however, the Buddha's essential teaching of "middle way" points to a balance between:

Wisdom & compassion — compassion is the vital "subjective" that guides technological wisdom towards the qualitative benefit of people.

Personal responsibility and independence, relationship with teacher and community — this emphasizes developing oneself to answer one's unique problems with support from others, rather than becoming dependent on the technology and expertise of a teacher or group of already advanced students.

Meaning and form — this emphasizes the timing of instruction and education about technology. More skills are not helpful if the student is not ready to digest and use them.

From a Buddhist perspective, we might reconceptualize "development aid" in terms of the way the aspirant follows the spiritual path. Through balancing head and heart, independence and interdependence, quantity and quality, a teacher does not solve students' problems, but empowers them to answer their own. In the same way, "development aid" as loans to increase material prosperity en masse can never **solve** the problems of a particular society. Rather such "aid" must be timely, aimed correctly, and geared dynamically towards the unique subjective factors of society.

As Buddhist practice begins to affect the inner core of the individual, transformation will manifest itself in the physical world. Initially, an individual's relationship to material goods and technology is radically altered, and he or she begins to relearn the meaning of simplicity and renunciation. Renunciation is not a shunning of the material world, but rather transforms our relationship with that world from the highly defined desires and "needs" of the maker and state to that which is necessary. Four such central necessities are food, clothing, shelter and medicine. Transforming a lifestyle of luxury into that which satisfies our needs means that we should be simple, frugal, and direct in our treatment of materials. As others depend on these for their livelihood as well, they are things to be taken seriously and not wasted or treated selfishly. In consumer society, we waste much time indulging in cuisine, fashion, interior decorating, and intoxication in drugs and alcohol. As we begin to see the material as **means** to building a mental and spiritual ecology, and not as **ends** for material growth, we begin to see the ease that it can create in our lives. Renunciation then becomes the practice of making our lives lighter and freer through material simplicity.

Beyond our relationship with the material, we obviously have emotional and spiritual requisites. These are the food, clothing, shelter and medicine for our spirits which give us sustenance towards reaching our higher goals. Humans have a fundamental necessity of connection, to feel comforted and nurtured by the world around them. The four material requisites provide this on a physical level. On the spiritual and emotional level, we also require comfort and nourishment. Life, society, and nature become three fundamental requisites for the individual to experience their interconnection with reality. In consumer culture, however, life has become the "needs" for personal indulgence in media, entertainment and technology; society the "need" for sex and consumer experience; and nature the "need" for environmental commodities.

As spiritual requisites, life becomes the process of self-discovery and self-knowledge through solitude, meditation or prayer, art and learning. Society becomes the way people connect and reaffirm their cooparative nature through proper partnership, family and community. Nature becomes the way all beings connect and this is practiced through a constant immersion where "environment" no longer exists as an idea indicating the separation of man from nature. In this way, the spiritual requisites extend the process of inner transformation and "development" outwards to society.

B) Personal Transformation Extends to the Social and "Structural"
The social, "structural" form of Buddhist practice is Sangha, the community of individuals who together following a process of internal transformation. Sangha incorporates individual practices on a larger scale to include:

Sociability, sense of fairness, sympathy and duty. Although the past two hundred years have done much to nurture freedom and equality in institutions, very little has been done for the fraternity and solidarity that hold societies together.

Human-scale collective. In which it is possible to encounter people face to face and within which people can feel comfortable.

An assertion of ethics. Without a strong sense of personal ethics, societies require an unacceptable level of policing and contracts; and without a strong sense of personal responsibility, it is inevitable that costs entailed will be a burden on our natural environment and our future generations.

From these fundamentals of individual and community transformation and development, we can begin to envision a new mandate for "development" that involves individual and community capacity building as the foundation for "structural development".

1. Education (wisdom)

For any structural improvements to be made in society there is the fundamental need to build the capacity of each individual and each community in a way which balances head and heart, independence and interdependence, and quantity and quality. The use of a buddhist style of "human resource develoment" which emphasizes communities and individuals coming to terms with their own needs and issues is an essential base for "structural development".

2. Culture (moral conduct)

For "development" to engender healthy societies, all facets of a society must be addressed, not simply the economic. Economic issues must be reprioritized within the overall structure of societies. This overall structure is what we can understand as "culture" which includes art, history, language, medicine and other aspects which combine to form healthy and self-sufficient societies.

3. Dynamics of Interrelation or Politics (concentration)

For individuals and communities to create the space for their own development, the dynamics for interaction must be clear and healthy. We have seen how structural reform has not changed the fundamental feudal nature of "developing" countries and that democracy is not a finished product in "developed" countries. More must be done to bring out cooperation and proper monitoring in political systems.

In such a way, the NGO movement has had a positive effect on the problem of community disempowerment in the "developing" world. They have done well on the second level of culture by reaffirming community values and bringing in other "soft or subjective factors" into the "development process". Their failures, however, have been in the first and third areas of education and interrelation. Firstly, their own inability to practice personal transformation amidst their structural agenda for "alternative" development has created organizations imbued with the same feudal patronage structures and megalomaniac personalities as their government counterparts. Further, as they have struggled for social space amidst the patronage systems of government, they have been unable to create proper horizontal connections with other NGO's and vertical connections with government and business sectors. However, a system of networking which is developing among NGOs, citizens groups, development agencies and even government offices suggests one alternative model.

This model is the network and one such example can be found in the Buddhist metaphor of Indra's Net. Indra's Net is a spider's web in which at each node appears a mirror which reflects all the other mirrors and vice versa infinitely. In this way, each infinitesimal part encodes all of the whole within it. From such a metaphor, we can envision a form of political organization which emphasizes:

a) Inter & independence in which power is not centralized but exists equally in every node. This of course presupposes the capacity of each individual and community as UNIQUELY empowered by the practice of internal transformation.
b) While emphasizing individual integrity, the whole is not the simple amassing of the parts. Rather, the interaction of the whole more strongly determines the nature of the parts. Relationship and connection between groups is thus vital, so there must be an emphasis on cooperation and communication.

This model of organization is being further explored in the work of quantum physics, particularly holographic models of the mind which posit a decentralized, multiple interactive model of the universe. Such a model puts a strong emphasis on the democratic and dynamic interplay of its parts and thus requires individuals to have their own critical perspective. Individuals and communities must be able to think for themselves, determine their own directions and development and then receive structural support in a timely manner. Such a model de-emphasizes the feudal power hierarchies with which development agencies have become partners in state run development projects. This framework is one still in the making and not without difficulties, yet contains principally clearer and more efficient decision making methods among groups.

C) Incompleteness of the Buddhist Model

An essential aspect of the Buddhist and quantum critique of the modern structural model is the insufficiency of any one approach, model or framework to answer all questions. In keeping with the pervasive dynamic of impermanence, we must continue to make adjustments to the models and frameworks we have developed according to the flux of causes and conditions. In this way, Buddhism and other movements which seem to oppose large development agencies like the World Bank and the IMF must also engage in their own internal critique.

One of the principal problems of Buddhist approaches to development has been precisely the inability to engage with development agencies and others involved in the important work of structural change in our societies. Typically, Buddhists have held up fuzzy models of a utopic small community as an answer to all our social ills. Yet, especially, in parts of the "developed" world like the U.S. and U.K., citizens' groups have been fighting passionately for the small government agenda which seeks to leave communities to themselves; however, they disregard the large number of people who are unable to fend for themselves and who are still dependent on government social support. The call for "small community", then, plays right into the conscious negligence by elites in "developed" countries to disregard the welfare of the whole. In such a way, Buddhists share the Bank's and other agencies' responsibility to develop new perspectives and a mutual dialogue of depth and understanding.

III. The Role of the Bank

The above presents some distance between the Bank's and the Buddhist approach to development. Each side has gaps in its approach which need to be filled in and perhaps supplemented by the other side. At the end of such an envisioning process, we must ask, "what can be done to enact change now?"

A) Policy Reform

The short term policy objectives for the bank and other major donor agencies remain problematic. If the Bank and such agencies truly wish to expand the scope of their work, they will have to contemplate their present limitations. The Bank and such agencies have an expertise in hard infrastructural development, and as lending bodies. It is therefore unrealistic within their mandates to suddenly become immersed in human resource development as personal transformation. Furthermore, is it truly in anyone's interest to borrow money for such programs?

These questions return us to the need to develop the languages and dialogues with a wider variety of social sectors and to explore the possibility of new frameworks for connection and cooperation, for example, the system of networking outlined above. In this way, the Bank could play a role in fostering more just relations between the various sectors of the "developing" societies it touches, across governmental, corporate, NGO and community lines. It has been witnessed that the Bank is exploring such ideas, for example, its proposal for "Research Capacity Building Through North-South Cooperation." For the mandate of poverty reduction to be realized, space must be created in society for the silent poor to articulate its own vision.

B) Internal Reform

At the same time, the existing structures that dominate social space and exhibit such a deterioration of moral standards must be confronted. This includes governmental offices, corporations, NGO groups and donor agencies such as the Bank itself. We have seen how modern structure building has neglected the transformation of individuals within these structures and how large structural bureaucracies inhibit the important communal factors for growth in personal connection and intimacy. Therefore, to begin the moral reform of corrupted structures we must shift our focus away from more structural reform towards the inferior transformation of the individual. Such practices have been outlined above and already exist in some of the brightest and most compassionate companies which understand that healthy workers do good work and that a healthy working community makes a successful business.

In order to aid the process of broadening perspectives and creating common languages, the notion of the "expert" must be expanded from those with abstract specialized knowledge to include those with an integrated knowledge of various fields and experiential knowledge from years immersed in the daily lives of donor communities. The "participatory development" trend is a timid step in this direction. Aid agencies must more aggressively develop staffs with a wide-range of experiences and knowledge who are intelligent as well as compassionate. Like the environment, an organization needs a bio-diversity of thinking and experiences in order to function in a healthy way.

Such an integration of staff with target communities can be an important step in creating mutual trust and respect. It can also be a critical step in redressing the one-way polemic of the "developed" helping the "underdeveloped" and in understanding what essential skills and knowledge the "underdeveloped" world offers the "developed". An "expertise" in "human resource development" skills such as renunciation, simplicity, and connection is probably one of them. In drawing on a final Buddhist metaphor, we might re-envision the Bank in the form of the traditional Buddhist "millionaire" (*setthi*) who is not known for how much she has, but for how much she **gives** to the community. Practicing the *parami* (perfection) of *dana* (generosity) she becomes well loved, rather than well endowed, for her forgiveness of all outstanding debt and her loaning of capital with no collateral or interest.

[This paper was prepared by a group of socially engaged Buddhists for the author to present to the President of the World Bank at Lambeth Palace in March 1998.]

THE CENTER FOR
SUSTAINABLE COMMUNITIES

Yesterday Susan George's presentation was so hopeful and inspiring. I have already been influenced by her books, especially *How the Other Half Dies* and *Faith & Credit: the story of the World Bank*. I was surprised however when Wolfensohn, the President of the World Bank, invited me with 8 other religious traditions to meet with him at Lambeth Palace last March. I was ready to quote Susan's book to attack him, but he asked for forgiveness and told us that the World Bank wanted to change drastically—not to support big infrastructure anymore. The Bank wants to work more with NGOs and to learn from various spiritual traditions. He asked me about the economic collapse in my country in July 1997. I said as a Buddhist that was a sign sent by heaven. In Buddhism, we called it a *devaduta*, heavenly messenger. They come to tell us that if we are mindful and skillful, we can overcome this crisis—indeed any crisis. But going to the IMF for help is not Buddhist. It means that we promote more globalization.

When Prince Siddhartha, the founder of Buddhism, saw an old man, a sick man and a dead man, he felt that these were heavenly messages. Hence, he left the palace to seek the truth. After six years he awoke from greed, hatred and delusion. That is when he became the Buddha, the awakened one, who overcame birth and death.

The President of the World Bank wanted me to be more specific, so I told him that globalization is of course synonymous with development and colonization. Although my country was not colonized politically, we were colonized intellectually and alienated from our Buddhist roots. Hence the Buddhist Kingdom of Siam has more prostitutes than monks, people have been uprooted from their villages. Bangkok, once a beautiful city—the so called Venice of the East—is now polluted and ugly.

People have been brainwashed by the World Bank and the American experts as well as by the Thai government to look down upon their indigenous cultures. Many of them have emigrated to the slums of Bangkok and abroad, or remain landless labourers on the land that was once theirs. They have become drug addicts, gamblers and superstitious.

Yet for the last decade or so, through Buddhist meditation, many of them have been able to empower themselves spiritually. Many of them are now able to cultivate rice without chemical fertilizers. They have started rice banks and buffalo banks—without going to the money lenders. To give is more important to them than to take. They have started cooperative movements at the grass roots level. They reintroduce traditional medicine and go back to local wisdom. The poor farmers have now organized into the Forum of the Poor with half a million farmers in membership. Last year they staged a nonviolent protest against the government for almost 3 months in Bangkok, and they outsmarted the prime minister. In the end he was forced to give them all the rights which have been denied to them for the last 3 decades.

I told the President of the World Bank that I intend to establish the Southeast Asian Center for Sustainable Communities. If the Bank wished to participate with us, they would be welcome. The mission of this Center is to help nurture spiritually and culturally appropriate development models for Southeast Asia. The Center will be based on a holistic understanding of development which promotes spiritual groundedness and values common to all religious traditions, the empowerment of participatory civil society, the conservation of indigenous and ethnic wisdom traditions, and the emerging ecological world view. A central feature of the Center will be its role as a demonstration, research and training institute in small-scale appropriate technologies, sustainable forestry and agriculture, ecological economics, and management skills for NGO's and small scale income generating activities. The Center will provide training in both new development projects as well as rehabilitation of degraded communities and ecosystems. The Center for Sustainable Communities will be the first major training facility in Asia to integrate the spiritual, cultural, ecological and technological aspects of sustainable development with the purpose of empowering communities from the grass-roots level.

The idea for the Center for Sustainable Communities grew out of the collaboration of a network of grassroots intermediary and regional NGO's who have been working together for the last 20 years under Sathirakoses-Nagapradipa Foundation (SNF). These are: Thai Inter-religious Commission for Development (TICD), Santi Pracha Dhamma Institute, Wongsanit Ashram, International Network of Engaged Buddhists, Komol Keemthong Foundation, Friends of the People, and many related groups. For the past 3 years this collaboration has been running year-round field education and residential training programs under the banner of the Spirit in Education Movement or SEM college, with courses such as Alternative Development, Deep Ecology, Conflict Resolution, Non-violent Action, Buddhist Economics, Alternative Politics for Asia, Art and Emerging Holistic World Views, Globalization and its Impact, Meditation for Social Action, and many others.

In 1996 SEM was asked to create the curriculum for a 3 months grass roots leadership training for religious leaders from an ethnic minority region in one of our ASEAN member states. The Training Program was composed of three main components. The first area was perspective development which included many of the SEM courses mentioned above. The second was exposure to different grassroots initiatives in Siam and the Philippines. The third part was skills training for NGO Management. This training proved to be very successful as most of the participants went back and started small scale community development projects with a participatory and bottom up approach based on their spiritual culture. Since then, we have been asked to run this course every year. Each training has two follow-up programs a year inside the country. At the end of 1997 we were also asked to run a similar training course for second rank leaders from the Forum of the Poor in Siam with a similar content. These people have been negatively affected by development projects of the government and big business corporations. For example many villagers have been relocated because of dam construction. We hope that this course will empower them to start appropriate development projects that are sustainable and take cultural values into serious consideration.

Between 1995-1997 our network was funded to build a program on spiritual alternatives to consumerism in Southeast Asia. This preliminary research resulted in a conference on alternatives to consumerism held in Siam in December 1997 which brought together over 200 regional spiritual leaders, NGO's and community leaders. At the conference they discussed participatory and appropriate scale development that would alleviate poverty without stimulating over-consumption. A network of 70 people are now actively engaged in identifying and documenting alternative cultural models and developing curriculum for use at village level.

From these experiences we have identified the need for a broader curriculum within the residential training for the Southeast Asian Center for Sustainable Development. The center will be a base for research, demonstration and longer training for grassroots leadership in the region. We found that throughout Southeast Asia, despite many decades of development, many communities of the poor, the marginalized and the minorities are still struggling for survival, cultural identity and autonomy. The younger leaders of these communities need to understand the present state of the world to put them in the right perspective as well as practical skills for participatory development as well as access to appropriate technology and small sustainable income generation activities. Once they are equipped thus they will be invaluable assets for their communities to mobilize local resources to alleviate poverty as well as build up an immune system to protect themselves from the destructive aspect of modernization. One aspect of this modernization is the consumer mono-culture which saps the life from their spiritual and cultural heritage. The lessons learned from the last 30 years of the NGO movement in the region prove that this aim is plausible and viable. We need to tap into these rich experiences and use them to create a desirable result.

The current indicators of success of the above programs are starting to manifest themselves. The first group of twenty trainees from our neighboring country are now one year on into their community development projects. Although working on different community projects they are facing and sharing challenges with each other and their peers. Their communities are tackling burning issues and together working out possible solutions to problems like food security, lack of education, hand to mouth living and debt. Their projects all have an element of self-reliance so as not to become dependent on outside funding with most becoming self-sufficient within three years. Projects include credit unions, community income generation, sustainable agriculture and leadership training. Many of the participants are Christian ministers and their experiences in Siam and the Philippines have become the basis for lively sermons that question the dominant development model and promote community and appropriate scale development.

In Siam engaged Buddhist projects are experimenting using meditation as a means for community awareness and imaginative reinterpretation of Buddhist traditions. One example is ordaining trees to stop them being felled. Buddhist monks and nuns are challenged and educated by SEM & TICD workshops that apply the Buddhist teachings to social work and conflict resolution.

The philosophy of the SE Asia Center for Sustainable Communities has a spiritual base and welcomes people from all faiths. All programs aspire to be culturally relevant to the diversity of ethnic/tribal cultures and participatory in all aspects. Gender awareness and sensitivity will be considered.

The demonstration technologies will be culturally appropriate and where possible made with parts available locally. They will be those that can help alleviate poverty without stimulating over consumption.

The programs will be grassroots oriented and help to build civil society by empowering leadership from the bottom up.

Ecological lifestyles and programs to restore and rehabilitate what has already been disturbed within our region will be encouraged, through teaching community development skills and environmental restoration technique and practices.

Specific Objectives

1. To enhance the capacity and effectiveness of grassroots leadership by strengthening a spiritual base and clarifying Asian values of community organizers and activists.
2. To offer grassroots leadership training to the poor, the marginalized and the minorities of SE Asia to build up their capacity to help their communities survive and retain their cultural identity and autonomy.
3. To create a demonstration center in small community development with organic agriculture and appropriate technology.

To use a bottom up, culturally appropriate approach in all activities.

Plan of Action

Land has been donated to enable SEM to build a much

needed year round facility and to extend its programe to serve the following groups: spiritual leaders who come to relate development to their spiritual traditions, grassroots NGO leaders and community organizers who are struggling to find appropriate development for their community tribal leaders, village headmen and women who are striving to keep their traditional self-reliant way of life. We will also feature occasional programs for the middle classes discontent with the consumer lifestyle and seeking ways of right livelihood.

The courses offered will draw from several broad areas of alternative education such as spirituality, holistic worldview, community skills development, and sustainable development in agricultural and small business methods.

To enhance the participants' feeling for their own spirituality we will offer spiritual walks, meditation, yoga and other contemplative practices. Broadening the students' perspectives will entail looking at holistic world views which are informed and open-minded with regard to world issues, and gender/race awareness. Deep ecology is also a part of broadening perspectives by examining and perhaps restructuring worldviews. Healthy communities are also a part of alternative education. Learning how to organize communities, use conflict resolution skills, and consensus decision making can help people lead happier, healthier lives and to avoid being so vulnerable to deceptive promises by big business in regard to development projects in rural, less organized areas. Rice banks and other locally run projects are sustainable and give a sense of well-being to those in a community. Finally, sustainable technology can improve the prosperity of communities and, indeed, nations without depleting the land and sapping the people's spirits. Some examples are: slope agriculture techniques, bio-intensive agriculture, composting techniques, food storage and preservation techniques, sustainable forestry techniques, well-drilling, and small-scale sanitation systems and primary/secondary water treatment systems. There are also other technologies that benefit the people in a direct way.

As requested by the President of the World Bank, I have sent this proposal to the World Bank in New York, with a copy to its representative in Bangkok. Hopefully we can further pursue the matter constructively in the near future.

[Delivered 6 September 1998, at the Conference, Expanding People's Spaces in the Global Economy, Finland.]

SUSTAINABLE LIFESTYLES
IN COMMUNITY

A Buddhist Perspective

I would like to begin with a quotation,

*"The existing system has taken the word sustainability
to its heart and now employs it at every turn but in a
context which deprives it of its meaning. For sustainability
is the most basic form of conservatism. It means not taking
from the earth, from the world, from society, from each
other, from life more than we give back. But when industrial
society uses the word, it means the sustaining of itself,
no matter what the cost. It means sustaining privilege, sustaining
poverty, sustaining abuse of the earth, sustaining inequality,
sustaining starvation, sustaining violence. To sustain the
existing system, to defend the status quo is neither conservative
nor sustainable. It is not even a status quo as a form
of continuous depletion or entropy. Such conservatism will
perish if it is not subjected to a radical revaluation."*

(Radicalism, Vintage, London, 1993, pp.96-7)

In "A Sense of Community", in **Resurgence** No.172, Geoff
Mulgan argues that Bookchin, Illich and Schumacher have reasserted
the primacy of small communities to take responsibility for their
own condition. Across a range of disciplines thinking has turned
to biology, the nature of living systems, and to principles of self-
organization as the only viable way to cope with change and
complexity. Mulgan says:

*"At the core of the idea of community are three basic
principles which are not only important, but also helpful
in thinking about a more sustainable politics for the next
century:*

"The first is the simple recognition of people's social nature and, one might add, of sociability, sense of fairness, sympathy and duty that evolutionary psychologists now see as hardwired into our genetic make-up. Two-hundred-years of history have nurtured institutions for freedom and equality but very little for the fraternity and solidarity that hold societies together. This softer value—a social capital that enables people to work together, to trust each other, to commit to common causes—has proved absolutely critical to societal success whether in narrow economic terms or in terms of well-being."

"The second principle is about scale. Community is deliberately a different word for society. It may refer to neighbourhoods or workplace, but to be meaningful it must imply membership in a human-scale collective: a scale in which it is possible to encounter people face to face...[and] to nurture human-scale structures within which people can feel at home. Social science is ill at ease with such ideas. Strangely, there is very little theory about the importance of scale in economics and sociology (unlike in biology where thinkers like D'Arcy Thompson long ago made the connection)."

"The third principle is a reassertion of ethics—the recognition that any viable politics needs to be prepared to make judgments about behaviour and about what types of behaviour work against the common interest and against the interest of future generations. Without a strong sense of personal ethics, societies require an unacceptable level of policing and contracts and without a strong sense of personal responsibility it is inevitable that costs will be shunted onto the natural environment and onto future generations...."

Buddhist Perspectives

In Buddhism, the spiritual community is known as *sangha*. A *sangha* should be small, autonomous and decentralized. The objective of the *sangha* is to live together in harmony with oneself, with the community and with one's natural surroundings; not to exploit oneself or other sentient beings. The lifestyle should be simple, content, self-reliant and mindful in order to restructure one's consciousness from selfishness to a state of greater selflessness, i.e. to overcome greed, hatred and delusion.

Once a member of the *sangha* can cultivate peace within, he or she can develop critical self-awareness to find how his or her potentialities can link together so they can reconstitute the community or communities to be harmonious and peaceful. Gandhi's ideas of the village republic are similar to the Buddha's ideas of *sangha*. Buddhadasa Bhikkhu said:

"*The entire cosmos is a cooperative. The sun, the moon and the stars live together as a cooperative. The same is true for humans and animals, trees and soil. Our bodily parts function as a coopertive. When we realize that the world is a mutual, interdependent, cooperative enterprise, that human beings are all mutual friends in the process of birth, old age, suffering and death, then we can build a noble, even heavenly environment. If our lives are not based in this truth, then we shall all perish.*"

In the Buddhist context, sustainable lifestyles are possible if people live in small communities, surrounded by natural habitats; the achievement of human freedom in community is possible when the individual's interests are in harmony with that of the whole.

In Buddhism, the basic teaching is the Four Noble Truths: The Truth of Suffering, the Truth of the Cause of Suffering, the Truth of the Cessation of Suffering, and the Truth of the Path to the Cessation of Suffering. Some monks and laity are trapped by consumerism and the social structure, they do not want to confront suffering and try to escape it. This can lead to a luxurious lifestyle which is harmful to oneself and others. People blindly adhere to such a lifestyle in the hope that one can perhaps be happy with material comfort.

Those Thai monks who are aware that they come from the poorest of the poor, who suffer more and more materially—not to mention legally and culturally—have now found out that the monkhood and the laity are interrelated. They want to help the laity to be liberated from suffering and a number of them do so in very meaningful ways.

I will quote a few instances to illustrate my point.(1) Surin, a very poor northeastern province has a large population of ethnic Cambodians. They were told by the government that they were second class citizens since they spoke Khmer more naturally than Thai. This came about when the name of the country was changed from Siam to Thailand in 1939 and especially since 1949. Until then the people were proud of their culture and language. Buddhist monks were their leaders, culturally, educationally, ethically and spiritually. They lived harmoniosly among themselves and other ethnic groups as well as with elephants and the forest.

Since the development decades of the 1960s onward, modern roads and electricity have reached Surin. Today, foreign tourists visit Surin to see the annual event of elephants playing football with the people. The result is that the Thai officials and the rich merchants benefit from the development policy and tourism, but the majority are much worse. Instead of being poor, many farmers in the area are now landless laborers on the land which was once theirs. They used to go to the forest for food and herbal medicine—now most of the forest is gone. Debt has driven them to drugs, gambling and superstition. They have lost all hope. They sell their children to be child laborers or prostitutes, and they remain no better off economically or socially.

Luang Po Nan, a local abbot, is an ethnic Khmer. He saw the suffering of the people who had been uprooted from their own culture and spiritual tradition. Being a meditation master and a charismatic leader, he persuaded his people to meditate together. Once they became mindful, they gained a sense of cooperation rather than competition. They are loyal to Siam and have lost their sense of inferiority in being ethnic Khmer. They have started farming together and stopped using expensive and harmful chemical fertilizers. They use buffaloes rather than tractors, so there is no need to buy petrol or borrow money to buy expensive machines. They have even started buffalo and rice banks. There is no need to go to money lenders anymore. Farming and harvesting have become joyful occasions of traditional song and dance. They have also formed a cooperative movement to help other villages and provinces as well as themselves.

In the early days the goverment wanted to put Luang Po Nan in jail because he talked about communal farming in his sermons. However, as a famous monk and meditation master, the local authority did not dare to touch him. Now the *sangha* has given him an ecclesiastical title, Khon Kaen University has given him an honorary doctorate, and last year the National Cultural Commission named him an exemplary citizen. Moreover, the non-chemical rice produced by his people is now sold directly to a Protestant group in Switzerland.

The people have become the community leaders and Luang Po Nan acts as a spiritual adviser.

(2) Also in the Northeast, Yasothorn is a new province that used to be part of Ubon. Here the people are mainly ethnic Lao rather than Khmer. Phra Khru Supa is a local abbot who works closely with lay people in Bangkok to persuade them to use traditional medicine for prevention, to cure illness and to take personal responsibility for health care. The people around his temple are proud to help him to increase the local production of traditional medicines as well as collaborating with the group in Bangkok.

Both Bangkok and Yasothorn have now gone on to produce rice and vegetables without chemical fertilizers. Another group called Greennet is promoting organic vegetables to the middle class of Bangkok who are happy to pay a little more than market price for healthy food. This not only helps the farmers in the Northeast, but also conscientizes the Bangkokians to realize that we are inter-related. We must fight nonviolently together for social justice and a healthy natural environment.

Recently a wider movement has been formed called Friends of the People. Membership includes the middle class in the capital as well as all the small farmers' associations in the North, the Northeast and the South of Siam.

(3) The Dewdrop Association, in the South, uses a bottom-up approach to work for the enviroment and social justice. Mr. Chuan Leekpai, the Thai Prime Minister, is from Trang where the project is based; however, he has little knowledge of the positive contribution of this association. In the last fifteen years, the Dewdrop Association has given real hope to the grass roots people in nearby provinces; a hope that had been destroyed in the name of national and economic development.

Also in the South is the People's University movement, which links grassroot teachers with monks and Muslim villagers.

These examples represent positive trends for the future of Siam. Some of these cases have been beautifully described by Sanidsuda Ekachai in her book, **Seeds of Hope**.

As for the monks, they have now formed themselves into a group called *Sekhiyadhamma*, i.e. how to apply the teachings of Buddhism in the modern world. They preach against fast food, junk food, the use of plastic and foam, chemical fertilizers, modernization or westernization without proper understanding of indigenous cultures and proper respect of the natural environment.

Of the 300,000 members of the Thai *sangha*, we have a core of around 300 in the *Sekhiyadhamma* group. This organization produces a quarterly journal of the same name that raises awareness of suffering, the cause of suffering and how to eliminate suffering though the Noble Eightfold Path of nonviolence.

Good friendship or *Kalayanamitta* is very important to this group. The Buddha said we need to have good friends and good companions. We can learn from others to develop ourselves and to help our society to be peaceful and just, starting with ourselves.

Once we can transform our consciousness to be less selfish, with help from good friends, we can transform our societies to be free from human oppression and exploitation. It may not be easy but it is possible.

The monks in *Sekhiyadhamma* are trying. No doubt we need many more good friends to help critically as well as collaboratively, so that, sooner rather than later, we can liberate ourselves and our fellow sufferers.

In Buddhism, one is taught to be aware of the three root causes of suffering: greed, hatred and delusion, which are fundamental blocks to openness, love, compassion and responsibility. As Bhikkhu Bodhi, an American Buddhist monk, has said:

> "*Desirous attachment sees the other as essentially desirable and seeks to draw him or her into one's possession or sphere of influence. Aversion, on the other hand, sees the other as essentially undesirable or even repulsive and attempts to remove the person from one's field of contact. Indifference is an attitude in which the other simply does not matter and his suffering and joys are of absolutely no consequence. In this way our relationships with others are limited to the manipulation of a few individuals who impinge on the domain of our personal concern, and the ignoring of all the many others who fall outside of that domain.*
>
> *The dominion of the ego in the emotional sphere appears most conspicuously in the weight of the unwholesome roots—greed, hatred, and delusion—as determinants of conduct. Because the ego is essentially a vacuum, the illusion of egohood generates a nagging sense of insufficiecy. We feel oppressed by an aching incompleteness, an inner lack requiring constantly to be filled. The result is greed, a relentless drive to reach*

out and devour whatever we can—of pleasure, wealth, power, and fame.in a never successful attempt to bring satisfaction. When we meet with frustration we react with hatred, the urge to destroy the obstacle preventing our satisfaction. If the obstructions to our satisfaction prove too powerful for the tactics of aggression, a third strategy will be used: dullness or delusion, an attitude of deliberate unawareness adopted as a shell to hide our vulnerability to pain."
(Bhikkhu Bodhi, "Nourishing the Roots",
Kandy, 1978. **Wheel** No. 259/260)

To be Buddhist can be helpful or harmful, depending on how you understand that term. If you want to practice Buddhism seriously, Thich Nhat Hanh advises us to take the first guideline: "Do not be idolatrous or bound to any doctrine, theory, or ideology, including Buddhist ones. Buddhist systems of thought must be guiding principles and not absolute truths".

There could be various Buddhist approaches to sustainable lifestyles in community. For me, freedom or liberation is basic, but it should not be merely Western liberalism. Bhikkhu Payutto explains that Buddhist freedom is threefold. First, people should enjoy basic freedom from all the fundamental insecurities and dangers that threaten their existence such as poverty or disease, and calamities such as drought or famine. Second, is the social freedom of being free from human oppression and exploitation. This involves tolerance, friendship and benevolence. The third, is the freedom of the inner life. This is freedom from mental suffering, from greed, hatred and delusion that corrupt the mind and cause people to commit all kinds of evil actions.

To achieve such states, we should utilize traditional training in *dana* (generosity) *sila* (moral) and *bhavana* (meditation or mindfulness). These practices must be done within the modern context. *Dana* does not mean just giving away what you do not want. It may begin in that way, but ultimately we give what is most dear—our life, our fortune and our fame. From a practical standpoint we should also give our thought and our time to those who really need them most.

By examining the practice of *dana* one can see that giving is more important than receiving. This is a radical departure from capitalism and consumerism because giving helps us to restructure our consciousness from selfishness to unselfishness. We should be content with a simple lifestyle, rather than accumulating wealth while others suffer. We should be willing to share our wealth, our talents, our time and our energy with those at the grassroots level. Once we restruture our mind to be humble, less ambitious and less selfish, we can start to transform our community to be more just, peaceful and environmentally conducive to all beings. Such a society would be full of goodness, beauty and truth.

The traditional practice of *sila* is useful in transforming the self and society. If we place the traditional precepts in a modern context, we see how transformation can take place. The Five Precepts, which constitute the basic guidelines of *sila*, entail a commitment to abstain from taking life, taking what has not been given, refraining from sexual misconduct, false speech, and intoxicants that cloud the mind.

If we understand liberation as an impulse which seeks to enhance life in all forms, then the Buddhist concept of *ahimsa* (non-killing) becomes a precondition for social liberation and world peace. To generate peace and bring about liberation requires eliminating, or at least reducing, violence. The problem is that there are several kinds of violence, as Johan Galtung reminds us. The clearest is direct violence as described in the first precept. However, there is also structural violence, violence that kills slowly because it is built into the very fabric of the social structures which create poverty, ecological imbalance, and death in the sense of a desperately unjust social structure that kills by giving disproportionately to the few in relation to the many. Isn't this form of violence included in the Five Precepts?

The second precept, abstaining from taking what does not belong to one also seems relevant here. Most of us are not involved in stealing, yet something is taken though there may not be an awareness of a theft.

From the above discussion one can conclude that Buddhism is a very strong ethical system that supports peace. Its precepts against violence represent a liberative impulse. However, there is a weakness; one may have a personal commitment against violence while at the same time remaining silent towards evil in society. The larger a social structure is, such as a nation-state or large corporation, or the merging of the two, and the more we become accustomed to it, the more violent it can become. Can Buddhists remain silent when the government continues to increase the national arms budget at the expense of basic health and education? Can a Buddhist keep silent when a multinational oil company constructs a gas pipeline in Burma at the expense of Burmese human rights and when the pipeline would destroy Thai forests? Some might argue that these issues are political rather than moral: they are both. The major question is exactly how the ethical inspiration of Buddhism can enlighten politics by being courageous enough to question such social structures, not merely the individual acts of people or their governments. If Buddhists understand structural violence and its roots in hatred (*dosa*) and learn how to eliminate violence mindfully and non-violently, then Buddhism will not only become relevant to the modern world, but also a source of its liberation. Similarly, consumerism is linked directly and indirectly to greed (*lobha*) and lust (*raga*). One can see this clearly in advertisements that exploit women's bodies to seduce buyers, artificially creating needs for certain products.

If Buddhists are to make a meaningful contribution to liberating the modern world from violence and oppression they must confront the three root causes of evil—greed, hatred and delusion—both individually as well as socially. All practicing Buddhists must develop right mindfulness. We must heighten our awareness of our limitations and restructure our selfish nature to become increasingly selfless. Moreover, we must create an inner peace along with an understanding of social realities and structural violence as a prerequisite for both individual and collective liberation. Full liberation is both individual and social.

In order to cultivate inner peace along with an understanding of social reality, one uses *bhavana* or meditation whose meaning might best be defined as 'self-training'. It does not mean merely sitting in solitude and engaging in some special form of internal contemplation, which is the image the word 'meditation' generally evokes in English. *Bhavana* means investigating, reflecting, learning, training or nourishing the mind in order to develop oneself towards enlightenment. *Bhavana* is thus the practice of mindful daily living.

The Buddha said that the most important requirement for true understanding of the self is to be calm in order to develop self-cultivation and self-criticism. Understanding is different from intellectual knowledge since it comes from both the heart and the mind. It helps one to be aware, to be humble, to know one's limits. At the same time, it promotes loving-kindness and compassion which enables us to empathize with others and to eliminate the cause of suffering.

In the face of greed, lust or delusion, *bhavana* is also a powerful tool to work against capitalism, consumerism, sexism, militarism and other socially degenerative forces. Self-awareness can also be used to criticize our own society, nation-state, culture and even our own religious tradition. With this attitude, one will utilize one's understanding to destroy oppressive systems.

Thich Nhat Hanh helps us in this context, he says;

> "In the Prajnaparamita, Heart Sutra, there's a term that can be translated as "Interbeing". Interbeing means that you cannot be a separate entity. You can only interbe with other people and elements. Interbeing is a good word. It might signify your true self. It is the awareness that you are made wholly of non-self elements. This insight is very important in the practice of psychotherapy. When a child has a problem and you treat the entire family, not just the child, you are applying the principle of non-self. The family members are not the child, but they cannot be separated from the child's problem. In order to help the child, the family must also be involved in the therapy."

> "When one looks at a flower deeply, non-flower elements are seen such as sunshine. Sunshine is not a flower but you cannot have a flower without it. Another non-flower element is garbage. Those who do not practice meditation may look at the flower and not see the garbage; however, after five or seven days, they'll see that the flower dies and becomes garbage. But those who truly see the nature of things do not need to wait for they see it immediately. When we look at garbage, we also see the non-garbage elements, we see the flower there. Perceptive organic gardeners see that even if they don't practice meditation. When they look at a garbage heap they see cucumbers and lettuce. That is why they do not throw garbage away, they keep garbage in order to transform it back into cucumbers and lettuce. If a flower can become garbage, then garbage can become flowers. This is the most important Buddhist teaching of non-duality. The flower does not consider garbage an enemy or panic when becoming garbage, nor does the garbage

become depressed and view the flower as an enemy. They realize the nature of interbeing. In Buddhist therapy, we preserve the garbage within ourselves. We don't want to throw it out, because if we do, we have nothing left with which to make our flowers grow."

(**Radical Conservatism**
TICD Bangkok, 1990, pp. 53-54)

With such awareness, one can see how consumerism operates as a secular religion to promise happiness in our world. As an English Buddhist put it:

"By participating in the sacrament of (luxury) purchase, sacrificing money, we buy more than an object. We also buy an image located within a system of images which we hold sacred. Purchase gives us a place within that system. When we buy a car we seek to acquire the power, prestige, sexuality, success, which the advertisements have succeeded in identifying with the car or whatever the commodity is. Consumerism works by identifying the sense of unsatisfactoriness or lack (dukkha) we all hold at a deep level of mind with a particular "lack" and then producing an object guaranteed to satisfy that need, resolve dukkha, provide happiness."

(David Arnott "The Individual and Society" in
**Buddhist Perception for Desirable Societies in the
Future**, TICD, Bangkok 1993)

As 'interbeings' we need good friends—kalayanamittas—because we cannot exist alone. The Buddha said that kalayana-mitta is most important external element for everyone. We need good friends, good company and friendships. From others one can learn to develop oneself and help society to be peaceful and just.

Another good friend, Maurice Ash, has just started the first Buddhist College in England. In his latest essay to mark his 80th birthday anniversary, he reminds us that, "far from accepting the world as it is, we have a commitment to reducing the scale on which society operates, to a scale on which morality can indeed be lived". He also says that holistic thought—being on the scale of our activities—points to the primacy of the local.

His essay has an appropriate title, which I would like to end my talk : "Beyond The Age of Metaphysics and the Restoration of Local Life." To sustain lifestyle in community, we must have good friends who care for the right scale, who understand that small is beautiful, stressing decentralization, local self-reliance and real participation of all, rather than the centralization of national government and multinational corporations with hierarchical systems which lead to monoculture.

[A lecture given at the Indian International Centre, Lodi Park, New Delhi 5 Feb 1998 and was published in *IIC Quarterly* Summer-Monsoon 1998.]

HEALING THROUGH
THE PATHWAY OF WISDOM

Concerns and Hope on Global Development for the New Millennium: A Thai Buddhist Perspective

At any International Conference, there are usually many wise words—and some not very wise words. All these words, however, have come mostly from our head. We have not paid much attention to our heart. May I therefore ask all of us to sit quietly for one minute—concentrating on our breath—the most important function of our life. If you don't believe me, stop breathing for five minutes! Indeed, we breathe in for the first time when we enter our mother's womb, and we breathe out the last time when we expire from this life. Yet we do not take care of our breath properly. So I would ask all of us to breathe mindfully, joyfully, peacefully for one minute. Through mindful breathing, you can synchronize your heart and your head. You can easily overcome anger, alienation and other deceptions. You can link the mundane world with the supramundane.

-1 minute silence-

If you don't like silence, you should try it again. If you like it, you can breathe mindfully more often.

Once we establish seeds of peace within, we can then develop critical self-awareness. We can transform ourselves from a selfish being to be more and more selfless. We can then see our society critically and meaningfully with a nonviolent and compassionate approach. We can then transform society to be peaceful and just, with environmental balance.

It is through breathing that one can learn to become mindful. This can lead to the practice of mindful living in daily life. One can practice this during every moment of one's life—while breathing, eating, drinking, washing the dishes, gardening or driving a car.

Once one practices mindfulness, one has peace and happiness inside and one can share that way of life with others. The present moment is a wonderful moment.

Traditionally, the first part of training the mind is to achieve *samatha* or a state of tranquility. This will allow us to plant seeds of peace within. The second is based on a technique for understanding the true nature of one's psychophysical constitution and of the world. This is called *vipassana* or insight meditation, which is an analytical method for exploring causal relations and problem solving. It develops into an internal factor for wisdom or right understanding by fostering detachment. In Pali, this is called *yonisomanasikara*, critical self-awareness, which leads to selflessness. Maintaining *yoniso-manasikara* helps one to be earnest. It helps generate energetic effort and it helps reduce selfish desire.

The Buddha said that the foundation for real understanding or wisdom (*pañña*) is equanimity to develop self-cultivation and critical self-awareness.

Wisdom is different from intellectual knowledge, since it comes from both the head and the heart. It helps one to be aware, to be humble, to know one's limits. At the same time, it promotes loving-kindness and compassion, allowing us to share the suffering of others and to work to eliminate its causes.

Of course, when one tackles the causes of suffering, especially in an oppressive social system, one usually gets hit by those who wish to maintain the status quo. Here mindfulness again helps one to understand one's danger and to forgive one's enemy.

The important thing is to bring out the awareness of one's anger in order to surround it with mindfulness. Then the anger is transformed into compassion. The Vietnamese monk, Thich Nhat Hanh, says that anger is like a closed flower. The flower will bloom when the sunlight penetrates deeply into the flower. If one keeps breathing and concentrating, mindfulness will infiltrate the anger. When sunshine penetrates a flower the flower cannot resist. It has to open itself and shows its heart to the sun. If one keeps breathing on one's anger, shining one's compassion and understanding on it, one's anger will soon crack and one will be able to look into the depths and see its roots.

One can deal similarly with greed, lust and delusion. Meditation is a powerful tool to work against capitalism, consumerism, sexism, militarism and the like.

Critical self-awareness can also be used to examine our own society, nation-state, culture—even our own Buddhist tradition. With this attitude, one will not hate the oppressors, the capitalists or the dictators. Yet one will use one's understanding to dismantle the oppressive system and its inherent violence.

I have been privileged to work for peace in Siam as well as to work with good friends in the International Network of Engaged Buddhists (INEB). The network is linked to the Buddhist Peace Fellowship in the U.S.A and with similar organizations in Europe and Japan—working to free ourselves from the root causes of suffering and to challenge the oppressive systems.

Despite social and political oppression and the destruction of the environment in Asia, my vision for renewing society and for human liberation is realizable because many of us work together as good friends or *kalayanamittas*.

The Buddha says a *kalayanamitta* is important for everyone. We need to have good friends, good companions and good friendships. We can learn from others to develop ourselves and to help our society to be peaceful and just, starting with ourselves.

When we can transform our consciousness to be less selfish with help from good friends we can transform our societies to be free from human oppression and exploitation. It may not be easy, but it is possible.

With critical self-awareness that helps us to change ourselves to be less selfish and to be non-violent and with good friends, we can look at our society and the environment with hope and encouragement to overcome social ills and environmental degradation.

To generate peace and to bring about liberation requires eliminating, or at least reducing, violence. The problem is that there are several kinds of violence. The clearest is direct violence as described in the first precept which states that five factors are involved in killing—not only life, but the perception of life, not only the thought of murder, but also carrying it out, and the result of death.

There is also structural violence, violence which kills slowly and is built into a social system. Of the five factors noted, only three apply here: there is life and the perception of life, but there is no thought of murder and no follow through. Death, however, is the result. But the result of what? Death does not result from direct violence but from a desperately unjust social structure that gives too much to the few and too little to the many. How does a modern Buddhist deal with this form of violece?

The second precept, abstaining from taking what does not belong to one, seems relevant here. Again the five elements are involved: someone else's belongings and awareness of the fact; the thought of theft and the act of carrying it out; and theft as the outcome. However, theft is not quite the same as structural violence. Something is taken, but there is no awareness of a theft.

A landowner has land, but the landless have only their ability to till the land. The landowner says "You may till my land, but you have to give me 70% of the harvest" (A figure fairly typical in most SEA countries). The landowner may feel he is being generous since the alternative is to use a tractor to till the fields. He may sell the land for a golf course at a tremendous profit. The peasant may feel grateful, for the alternative maybe starvation or selling his daughter as a prostitute or migrating to a city to work as a cheap labourer.

Surely there is something morally wrong in this arrangement. To maintain an oppressive structure of this kind something else is needed. The usual capital "B" Buddhist explanation of the law of *karma* is that the peasants are now reaping the results of their bad deeds committed in the past while the landlord obviously cultivated much merit by building temples and Buddha images. Hence both the rich and the poor must support the material aggrandizement of the monkhood for the future welfare of each other.

Buddhism with a small "b" is certainly against this kind of deceptive teaching. If the landlord practices *dana* (charity or generosity), he will feel it is wrong to get 70% out of the land, while the landless labourers lack enough to live on. Buddhadasa's Dhammic Socialism is an approach that emphasizes not taking more than is needed and is in accordance with the laws of Nature, since people would share whatever extra they have out of compassion and loving-kindness. People would set aside for themselves only what they needed, anything in excess of that would be left for society.

A third type of violence, known as cultural violence is any element in the culture, particularly religion or ideology, that legitimizes direct and/or structural violence. One can see it very clearly in the mass media, especially in advertising. Of course, there are Buddhists past and present, and there will be some in the future, who commit direct violence and participate in structural violence. They will not, however, find any support for this in the Buddhist scriptures. To claim this support would be a violation of the fourth precept which is against false speech. Although that precept is more concerned with lying in the conventional sense than in legitimizing violence, if Buddhism is invoked in defense of violence it constitutes an act of lying.

From the above arguments, one can conclude that Buddhism contains a very strict ethical system supportive of peace. Its precepts against violence represent a liberative impulse. But there is a weakness: strength in personal commitment is combined with the silent mechanisms of evil. The larger a structure is, such as a nation state or a large corporation, or a merging of the two, the more we become accustomed to it, the more violent it becomes. Can a Buddhist fulfill the obligations of military service? Should Buddhists remain silent when the government continues to increase the national budget for military armaments at the expense of basic health and education? Some might argue these issues are more political than moral. Of course, they are both. The major question is exactly how the ethical inspiration of Buddhism might enlighten politics by being courageous enough to question a socially unjust society—not merely the individual acts of people or their government.

If Buddhists understand structural violence and its roots in hatred (dosa) and learn how to eliminate it mindfully and nonviolently, Buddhism will be a source for social liberation in the modern world. Similarly, consumerism is linked directly or indirectly to greed (lobha) and lust (raga). One can see this clearly in advertisements and mass media, which exploit woman's bodies to artificially created need.

Modern education deals almost exclusively with the heads, not the hearts, of students. The clever ones are recognized and rewarded materially and financially, although they need not be generous or aware of social ills. Most of the rich and powerful are not happy. Their exalted positions rest directly or indirectly on mass poverty and ecological destruction. This is indeed ignorance (avijja) or delusion (moha).

If Buddhists are to make a meaningful contribution to world peace or the liberation of the modern world from violence and oppression, we must confront the three root causes of sufferings which are found not only in the individual but also in the structure of society. Therefore, these roots of evil must be dealt with by

Buddhists. The moral precepts must exist not only for moralists. All practicing Buddhists must develop right-mindfulness.

Right-mindfulness leads to wisdom, one is able to see things as they really are. They are not seen from our prejudicial views or compartmenalized; they are not only seen from a logical viewpoint. Social engineering alone could not solve real problems—as all problems are inter-related.

Thich Nhat Hanh explains in this way,

"In one sheet of paper, we see everything else, the cloud, the forest, the logger. I am, therefore you are. You are, therefore I am. We inter-are."

He went on to say,

"I know that in our previous life we were trees, and even in this life we continue to be trees. Without trees, we cannot have people; therefore, trees and people inter-are. We are trees and air, bushes and clouds. If trees cannot survive, humankind is not going to survive either. We get sick because we have damaged our own enviroment, and we are in mental anguish because we are so far away from our true mother, Mother Nature."

Buddhist teachings provide a means of evaluating the nature and direction of global development. The significance of the approach is that it entails a consideration of the extent to which social and economic policies tend to contribute to or diminish human suffering. This aspect is often obscured in the quest for modernization and westernization.

The present course of economic development has enhanced disparities in wealth, depleted natural resources, devastated the environment and alienated people from their culture. It is directed by the profit motive embodied in the corporate culture and is oblivious to the extent of the discontentment of people.

Buddhism teaches that the causes of suffering are linked directly with greed, hatred and delusion. These conditions remain unbridged in contemporary society and have produced a consumer culture in which the dominant value is the acquisition of goods. The earth vision of the new millennium requires that we rediscover the spiritual values embodied in our cultural traditions. The despair that characterizes our civilization is a product of our having forgotten the interrelatedness of our being.

For the future to be possible, we need an individual recognition of freedom and responsibility as well as a bottom-up kind of development. I am happy to inform you that in my country, the people at the grassroots who suffered from the maldevelopment policies of the goverment, the World Bank and the IMF, during the last three to four decades, have now empowered themselves spiritually. They farm together, joyfully, traditionally, without chemical fertilizer and they form themselves into various cooperatives to demand their rights, to have alternative development with self-reliance. Some of the middle-class in my country have learned from the suffering poor and they now join hands in a new movement. And this could really be seeds of hope for many of us.

I am aware that healing through the pathway of local and indigenious wisdom is very difficult, yet I was encouraged when I read President Vaclav Havel's writing, especially when he said:

> *"We must not be afraid of dreaming the seemingly impossible, if we want the seemingly impossible to become a reality."*

> He went on to say, *"it is well known, for instance, that enormous private multinational corporations are curiously like socialist states; with industrialization, centralization, specialization, monopolization, and finally with automation and computerization, the elements of depersonalization and the loss of meaning in work become more and more profound everywhere. Along with that goes the general manipulation of people's lives by the system (no matter how inconspicuous such manipulation may be, compared with that of the totalitarian state)."*

Kirpatrick Sales said in his book **Rebel Against the Future**, that the Industrial Revolution in England during the last century destroyed the British farmers for the benefit of the landlords and the industrialists, for the growth of capitalism and the expansion of the empire. He also said that the new empire of globalization run by the transnational corporations and their megatechnology and computers will make more members of the middle class jobless within two decades.

Indeed globalization is a new demonic religion. It uses the media to create a sense of lack. Hence we are driven to earn more in order to acquire more, yet we can never reach a point of contentment. Since globalization is under the control of the big corporations, the media is used to direct us blindly toward the monoculture of more and more technology, of the McWorld of fast food, junk food, the cola and jean syndrome.

But if we follow the First World lifestyles there will not be sufficient natural resources for all of us. Most of us will not be happy with this style of life that is harmful to ourselves, our family, our society and our natural environment. If however, we follow the indigenous people's way of life, we can all live simply and have time to enjoy ourselves and to become part and parcel with the community as well as with our mother earth.

I want to stress the importance of the indigeneous people, such as the Roma in Europe, the Native Americans, the Aboriginals in Australia, the Maori in New Zealand and the many minority ethnics in Asia, whose members are not usually represented at any International Conference.

Indeed the indigenous peoples still suffer a great deal, yet they can teach us that we need to opt for local and indigenous wisdom and not the monoculture of globalization. Our decision making must invoke more than the limited rationalism and pragmatism that have caused us to become more and more compartmentalized.

We should learn from the indigenous people about the wholeness of life and the sanctity of the natural order. We should learn to be alone with nature, to live with birds and deer, to appreciate and respect nature. Through this understanding, we can realize that intellectualism and social engineering cannot liberate us from suffering.

We need to return to the best of our spiritual traditions, to shamanism, mythology, traditional rituals, songs and dances—to experience life as it is available and alive in many indigenous communities that are being threatened by corporate entities which are supported by states in the G8 and elsewhere in derogation of the interests of their own people and natural resources.

For corporations, natural resources are only a source of economic gain. When one area has been exhausted they will move to another. The people are relevant only to the extent that they serve to generate income either as laborers or consumers. Money is less important for the indigenous people. Of greater significance to them and for us is to live happily with dignity, with a sense of the sacred, and with a spiritual dimension to our lives This means to be in harmony with the earth, revere our ancestors, and respect our communities with a commitment to the generations to come.

If we care for our survival, we must not only question the G8 economic policies but the policy structures that have emerged which are no longer accountable to indigenous people. We must also question the legal and judicial systems that maintain the status quo.

We need alternative economic and political strategies designed, like E.F. Schumacher says, "*as if human beings matter.*" Indeed, we need alternative educational programs which encourage us to integrate the manifold aspects of our being. We must be able to link our head with our heart so that we escape compartmentalization and develop the capacity to grow seeds of peace, joy within ourselves. We will bring about change through this process. Not by hating the oppressors, but by challenging structural violence. Through non-violence we can seek a transformation to create a just and peaceful world.

We must also challenge Scientism (not Science), which refers to the narrow minded and dogmatic application of scientific methods to all fields of knowledge. Scientism has developed out of the Enlightenment period in Europe during the 17th and 18th centuries. Scientism has based itself in a reliance upon the rational human mind to observe and understand all aspects of reality. As such, there has been a great focus on the material and quantitative, for what is spiritual and qualitive is irrational. What is irrational is out of the bounds of scientific inquiry, private to the individual and ultimately of little value to the organization of society. Such a focus has given birth to the "idea" of machine which measures and produces material quantities. Beginning with the Industrial Revolution, this mechanization process has not only transformed the way we produce and consume material goods, but also the way we view ourselves, organize our societies, and inter-relate. Scientism is thus a misuse of scientific methods in the realm of human relationships such as psychology, politics and economics.

The machine has transformed our understanding in each of these areas. Man's essential nature has become the sum of his appetites. Man's society has become the state, a political machine which collects quantitative duties (taxes) and distributes quantitative needs (housing, roads, utilities). Thirdly, man's market place has been stripped of its place and thus differing qualities have become the sole trading of material desires. With market values, such as acting in one's own interests, competitive behavior, subordination of personal relationships, and anonymity being unleashed into society as a whole, the individual becomes free to pursue appetites and competition for greater shares. This mechanization of man which has become a social norm has produced an all-encompassing ethic of "progress" during the colonial period and "development" in the post World War II period. These terms are always expressed in quantities such as GNP, literacy rate, doctors per square kilometer, etc. Yet the nature of such a system is to disregard diversity in the search for universal principles to organize the whole. The whole becomes greater than its parts (organism). The consequence is that local particularities and the diversity of the whole system is broken. All constituents are stripped down to common sets of quantifiable properties under this homogenization. What we are faced with today are the smaller communities, regions, ethnicities and countries stripped of their own powers and made dependent on technologies prescribed by the "scientists" of larger states and markets.

Buddhist teachings offer a radically different approach to understanding humanity (as opposed to organizing humanity). The overall concept may be called Dharma, which has a deep and wide range of meanings. Strictly, Dharma is Nature—its laws, duties and fruits. It is not a system for streamlining, organizing or managing reality as Scientism is, but rather an organic Truth with its own organizing systems which humans come to understand. In certain respects, Dharma is a science of observing and discovering the laws and properties of an object. However, it encompasses not only physical and biological laws but also psychic and karmic (causality) laws. In this sense, it opposes Scientism by working with the spiritual as well as the material. Further, the spiritual is not reduced to measurable quantities but rather the direct experience of qualities. As such, the emphasis is not upon machine but on sentience, on the living quality of any phenomenon. This sense for quality is also a sense for value and meaning which contrasts the pure quantification of Scientism. In Scientism, man moves forward for knowledge of all phenonmena. Much of this knowledge may have little meaning or digestibility for most people. Dharma, however, moves man forward for knowledge in the service of wisdom. Knowledge fits into a search for meaning and relevance and only certain kinds of knowledge are acquired at certain times as the individual or group may find use for them. The aim of Scientism is to clarify as much as you can at once. Dharma uses each piece of knowledge as a step towards greater understanding of self, society and Nature. Dharma has a unique quality for each person and place. It respects the law of natural diversity in which forms find their highest possible development through access to a fantastic array of sources. In this way, Dharma fits into the concept of ecology where the parts form an equally important part of a larger whole. Further, Nature or Dharma is not just the nature of the woods or ocean but the nature of all phenomena, such as the diverse properties of the mind. Understanding and harnessing these properties of Dharma provides a meaningful freedom. This is a freedom not to pursue what one wants but to discover one's full potential. Knowledge of this freedom, however, also bequeaths a sense of duty and responsibility: duty and responsibility to those forces which enable and enhance one's freedom. This is duty to oneself, to supporting the Truths of Nature. Within such an order, the mass of artificial needs dictated by state and market transform into a clear and simple group of requirements for achieving this qualitative freedom. Dependence upon technology is replaced by the independence of free-inquiry and the inter-dependence of self, society and Nature.

Scientism stands in opposition to the established religions with rigid institutions and dogmas. Now there is a new scientific approach to the living universe which produces a new kind of scientist who is humble and relies upon his or her heart as well as head. This science links beautifully with the best in spiritual endeavor and can help us appreciate the wholeness of being.

I have attempted to approach this new trend of develpoment through projects which redirect us to a consideration of the spiritual dimension of existence.

Alternatives to Consumerism is a project which recognizes that we must confront the new demonic religion and strive to re-establish standards of value derived from the community. Gatherings are organized which afford people from diverse communities the opportunity to exchange stories and share experiences.

The Spirit in Education Movement is an educational project that seeks to integrate spiritual teachings into our understanding of the world. It offers an alternative to the narrow unconnected approach of modern education. These projects are informed by the fundamental wisdom of the noble truths. They demonstrate the manner in which the application of wisdom to social conditions can generate justice, peace and ecological balance. I hope that we are together in this venture. We need a movement against globalization by the transnational corporations and toward the reliance upon local culture and communities if we are to live harmoniously together with understanding and love.

[for The Twenty-first International Conference on the Unity of the Sciences, Washington D.C. November 24-30, 1997.]

VALUE CRISIS IN THE WEST
AND IN THE EAST

An Engaged Buddhist's Perspective

Buddhism teaches that all sentient beings have the capacity for enlightenment. Defilements of consciousness—greed, anger, and delusion—may, however, obscure the path to personal liberation. Perhaps no course of conduct so clearly exemplifies the manner in which the human spirit can be misdirected by greed, anger and delusion as does the consumerism which dominates much of contemporary society.

In a commodity based society, profits are dependent upon the consumption of goods. It is therefore not surprising that the transnational corporations that control many aspects of our society promote an ethos that equates the act of purchasing with the process of becoming an actualized being. This manifestation of corporate greed is enacted through pervasive propaganda and embodied in the implicit values of contemporary social institutions.

The imposition of these values is successful because individuals have become alienated from their culture and from each other. The sense of community that led people to share scarce resources and work cooperatively has been supplanted by an anger or competitiveness that causes people to seek acquisitions at the expense of their neighbors.

At the most profound level, consumerism owes its vitality to the delusion that people maintain about themselves and their relationship to nature and other beings. For the Buddha, it became clear that the "self" constituted only a pattern of persistently changing experiences which had no more substance or permanence than those experiences.

We are deluded into seeking some transcendental subject,

something that defines experience yet lies beyond that experience. We are exhorted to know thyself and yet the self in this dualistic system remains unknowable. The delusion of the autonomous individualized self is, for the Buddhist, the fundamental cause of suffering. Ontologically, we become estranged aspects of our experience of ourselves and others and are precluded from any meaningful conception of identity.

Consumerism provides an artificial means of defining our existence by suggesting that we arrive at a sense of identity through the process of acquisition. It becomes a perverse corollary to the Cartesian proof of personal existence. "I shop therefore I am."

I have often referred to consumerism as a demonic religion because of the manner in which individuals become entrapped in a cycle of behavior that is fundamentally self-defeating. In embracing consumerism one accepts an insatiable desire for goods as a means of self-realization. It is a practice which ultimately leads to despair.

The deterioration of the community as a significant, social, economic and political system is both a cause and a consequence of consumerism in our contemporary culture. Traditional communities in both the East and the West, the North and the South, were predicated upon a recognition of the interrelationship of all beings and the responsibilities that arise from that relationship. Industrialization tended to undermine the conditions upon which the community was constituted. The exaltation of wealth and possessions often led to a disintegration of the community. Therefore, the individual, isolated within the society, grasps at the new sense of purpose configured by the corporate culture.

For the engaged Buddhist, the hope that exists for our civilization comes from the prospect that we may someday bring about a reinstatement of the decentralized institutions and values of the community. The recognition of our interdependence is not in Buddhism an abstract philosophical axiom to be arrived at deductively, but rather a lesson one learns from mindfully attending to our experiences. These lessons may be taught by our good friends, kalayanamittas, our families, and the members of our community. Through these associations we come to understand compassion and the commonality of our being. We learn to act unselfishly and to forgo the suffering that comes from vain attachments.

The engaged Buddhist is not, however, a romantic reactionary seeking refuge in the past. The Buddhist, perhaps more clearly than most, recognizes the inevitability of change. The social matrix which creates the community is impermanent and historically conditioned. Some organizational structures will be inappropriate for contemporary needs. In some instances, the community may have been predicated upon principles or conditions which have, unlamentably, become obsolete, such as patriarchy, authoritarianism, and physical or social isolation. The community cannot be reinstated by the imposition of superseded values' which were dependent on the conditions of a closed society.

This represents the fundamental challenge to the engaged Buddhist. How does one re-establish the sense of interdependence and mutuality of the community in a form that is adapted to the exigencies of contemporary conditions? This is not a subject to be approached through theoretical speculation, but rather through an examination of the actual history and experience of people in social organizations. For this reason an organization with which I am affiliated, coincidentally called "Alternatives to Consumerism", offers international conferences where people who have confronted the destructive impact of consumerism relate accounts of their struggles. One of the most edifying of these accounts has been the story of the southern fishing villages in my country, Siam.

In Siam the southern villages along the Andaman Sea traditionally survived as fishing communities. The depletion of the mangrove forest and excessive exploitation by large commercial fishing ventures in recent years served to virtually destroy the livelihood of the local fisherfolk. Many were forced to migrate to the cities but some organized and found strength in their traditional culture. Villages from twelve provinces united together and organized the "Federation of Southern Local Fisherfolk." They documented the practices which were illegally devastating the fishing ground and demonstrated the efficacy of simple methods of environmental protection. Ultimately, the governmental agencies were forced to take action.

The agencies proposed that each village be afforded the opportunity to control the fishing grounds immediately adjacent to it. The government was shocked when the villagers rejected this solution. The fisherfolk realized that this territorial form of organization would result in small, competing groups and would destroy the unity that they had achieved. Through their efforts at organizing, they had come to recognize that their communities were no longer defined territorialy but in terms of a commonality of interest. Acting together, the villagers created a broader and more inclusive concept of the community which was more consistent with their contemporary needs. Their strength emerged from the appreciation of their interrelatedness. They sought uniform regulations that would preserve the food resources for all the villages.

The essential characteristic of the community is its principle of inclusion. As we become more attuned to compassion as the instrumentality of social organization, we can embrace the community.

So it has been with the small scale fisherfolk who first became aligned with each other and then came to recognize their affinity with others facing oppressive conditions. They have now joined forces with the Forum for the Poor, an organization composed mainly of impoverished farmers from the northeastern part of the country creating a larger and more diverse community.

It is perhaps ironic that I have chosen the southern fisherfolk as an example of engaged Buddhism because the villagers are mostly of the Muslim faith. They have exhibited Buddhism with a small b—the recognition that we are sustained by the values which emanate from compassion which is, I believe, a core concept of all great religions.

For the engaged buddhist, the community is a source of value. These values serve not merely to create a just society but also to provide the conditions for personal liberation. Functioning in the community and participating in the public sphere we are afforded an opportunity for personal transformation as we become less self-involved and more mindfull of the interconnectedness of being. Likewise when we engage in individual spiritual practice we create the conditions conducive to the establishment of the community. Social transformation must begin with ourselves; Buddhism provides a path to this transformation.

In addition, when one tackles the causes of suffering, especially within an oppressive social system, and encounters resistance and retaliation from those who wish to maintain the status quo, *bhavana* helps to understand this danger and to forgive one's enemies.

Bhavana is a powerful tool against all forms of suffering both within oneself and within the environment. As Thich Nhat Hanh has repeatedly pointed out, mindful breathing is a tool which can be used to surround feelings of hatred, greed and delusion which arise within oneself, shining *metta* onto these feelings until they crack and make it possible to look into their roots. At this point the mind is unable to resist flowering, just as a flower is unable to resist blossoming when the sun shines into its heart. At the social level, *bhavana* can also be used to work against capitalism, consumerism, sexism, militarism and the many other 'isms' which undermine the wholesomeness of life. It is a tool for criticizing positively and creatively our own society, nation state, culture and even our own Buddhist tradition. With this attitude, we do not fall into the traps of hating our oppressors but are able to use understanding to destroy the oppressive systems and violent structures.

His Holiness the Dalai Lama has provided an inspiring model for many of us to continue to oppose evil and oppression while cultivating seeds of peace within and maintaining love for our enemies. I am convinced that one day Tibet will be free from Chinese domination and destruction. Perhaps at that time it will offer us an example of Buddhist democracy or "Dhammic Socialism". Similarly, I am convinced that the moral courage of Aung San Suu Kyi will one day free the peoples of Burma from the SLORC military junta.

I was privileged to work with the Ven. Maha Ghosananda, who was recently nominated for the Nobel Peace Prize, in the Khmer refugee camps after the Americans abandoned Cambodia to the Khmer Rouge and later the Vietnamese invasion. He was working in the camps to establish peace among the several violent factions. It was very hard, but the Venerable was determined. He also asked us to conduct reconciliation workshops using meditation among rival Khmer monks and lay people. He led quite a few peace walks through the war zones. We have worked similarly with people from Burma, Nepal, Bangladesh and Sri Lanka.

I have also been privileged to work for peace and to challenge structures of oppression in Siamese society and in other parts of the world, as well as with *kalayanamitta*, good friends, in the International Network of Engaged Buddhists which is linked to the Buddhist Peace Fellowship as well as with similar organizations in the United States, Europe and Japan. We have also recently formed Kalayanamitra Council to help the suffering Burmese peoples vis-a-vis the Yadana pipeline from Burma to Siam. We hope the Council will also raise the awareness of the Thai people to take action for human rights in Burma as well as for ecological balance in their country. Despite social and political oppression and the destruction of the environment in this region, my vision for renewing society and for human liberation is partially sustained by the support and community of working with *kalayanamittas*.

According to the Buddha, *kalayanamittas* are the most important external elements for everyone. We need to have good friends, good companions, and good friendship so that we may learn from others in order to develop ourselves and our societies towards peace and justice. We start with peace and justice within ourselves. Once we can restructure our consciousness to be less selfish then, with *kalayanamitta*, we can surely reconstitute our societies to be free from oppression and exploitation. This may not be easy, but it is possible.

This development goes beyond the human rights conventions and points to a positive direction beyond the simple (or not so simple) eradication of evil. The eradication of evil is meant to provide a groundwork for the development of a fuller, more spiritual life; for a reintregration, in Taoist terms, into the higher levels which were lost before the discussion of justice was ever necessary.

[A keynote address at INEB's annual conference in 1993.]

GOD FROM
A BUDDHIST VIEWPOINT
A Theravada Response to Christian Upāya

I

The term *upāya* is a classical Mahayana term that also occurs in the Theravada canon incidentally or in late texts. The *Nikāyas* speak of three kinds of skill: skill in entering (*āya*), skill in learning (*apāya*), and skill in means (*upāya*).

It is clear that this terminology refers to the spiritual attitude of a *bhikkhu* or *bhikkhuni* who is trained to be an expert in the management of his/her practice on the path of enlightenment. In the *Suttanipāta*, it is the expert boatman who takes others across a swift stream, he is described as a 'skillful knower of the means'.

It is remarkable that *upāya* refers to the activities of both an aspiring monk or nun as well as a good teacher who is skilled in the ways of helping others across spiritual thresholds.

Other Pāli usage is either non-technical, late or incidental. In the Theravada *Pāramitās* (perfections), *upāya* is not one of the ten qualities leading to Buddhahood. They are 1) giving (*dāna*), 2) morality (*sīla*), 3) renunciation (*nekkhamma*), 4) wisdom (*paññā*), 5) energy (*viriya*), 6) patience (*khanti*), 7) truthfulness (*sacca*), 8) unshakable resolution (*adhiṭṭhāna*), 9) loving-kindness (*mettā*) and 10) equanimity (*upekkhā*).

These Parāmitas were developed and matured by the Mahabodhisattva Shakyamuni in his past existences and his realization of them demonstrated in many of the *Jātakas* which, only the verses are regarded as canonical.

In the **Vissudhimagga**, a classical Theravadin text, it is said that through developing the four sublime states of loving-kindness (*mettā*), compassion (*karunā*), altruistic joy (*muditā*) and equanimity (*upekkhā*), one may reach these ten perfections:

> As the Great Beings are concerned about the welfare
> of living beings, not tolerating the suffering of beings, wishing
> long duration of the higher states of happiness of beings,
> and being impartial and just to all beings, therefore 1) they
> give alms (dāna) to all beings so that they may be happy,
> without investigating whether they are worthy or not. 2)
> By avoiding to do them any harm, they observe morality
> (sila). 3) In order to bring morality to perfection, they
> train themselves in renunciation (nekkhamma). 4) In order
> to understand clearly, what is beneficial and injurious to
> beings, they purify their wisdom (paññā). 5) For the sake
> of the welfare and happiness of others, they constantly exert
> their energy (viriya). 6) Though having become heroes
> through utmost energy, they are nevertheless full of for-
> bearance (khanti) towards the manifold feelings of beings.
> 7) Once they have promised to give or do something, they
> do not break their promise in truthfulness (sacca). 8) With
> unshakeable resolution (adhiṭṭhāna) they work for the weal
> and welfare of beings. 9) With unshakeable kindness (mettā)
> they are helpful to all. 10) By reason of their equanimity
> (upekkhā) they do not expect anything in return.
>
> (**Vsm.** IX24)

I quote the **Visuddhimagga** to describe the misconception
of those who claim that Theravādins are Hīnayānists, solely caring
only for their own liberation.

In Mahāyāna schools of Buddhism, the six pāramitās do not
include *upāya*. They are liberality, morality, patience, energy, meditation
and wisdom. It is only later that four more perfections were added
as auxiliaries, namely *pranidhāna* (vows for bodhi and service),
upāya (skillful means), *bala* (strength or purpose) and *jñāna* (knowledge).

The relative inattention to the term *upāya* in Pāli texts and
the later addition in Mahāyāna texts does not mean that the way
of thinking assumed in this terminology is foreign either to Theravāda
Buddhism in its fully developed form or to early Buddhism.

Admittedly, there is no direct evidence that the Buddha
himself made use of this specific term to explain the way his teaching
was to be understood. Nevertheless, there are many indications that
his message was presented with a conscious pragmatic skill.

The well known scriptural similes such as the raft, the poisoned arrow, and the water snake in which the provisional and practical nature of the Buddha's teaching is made clear, support the relevance of *upāya* to Buddhism. The Buddha did not provide an explanation to all the metaphysical problems that interest mankind. He explained what he thought was necessary to alleviate *dukkha* and not to satisfy curiosity. It is a means of deliverance and a doctrine of reality in which every encouragement is given to investigate the riddle of life. It is not necessary to indulge in idle speculation or theorizing, nor is faith demanded as a first cause.

This knowledge does not bring us any nearer to the goal, it only gratifies childish curiosity. Although other religions teach about life's beginning, Buddhism does not speak about the first cause of life. Nevertheless, it emphasizes cause and effect with regard to a life continuum according to the doctrine of Dependent Origination (*paticca-samuppāda*).

The doctrine of Dependent Origination leads one to the final goal of *nibbāna* or liberation which is defined as "...unborn, unoriginated, uncreated, unformed. If there was not this Unborn, Unoriginated, Uncreated, Unformed, escape from the world of the born, the originated, the created, the formed would not be possible," (*Udāna* VIII 3)

However, one cannot too often and emphatically stress the fact that not only for the actual realization of the goal of *nibbāna*, but also for a theoretical understanding of it, it is an indispensable preliminary to fully grasp the truth of *anattā*, egolessness, and insubstantiality of all forms of existence. Without this understanding, one will misconceive *nibbāna*—according to either one s materialistic or one's metaphysical learning—either as annihilation of ego, or as an eternal state of existence within which an ego or self enters or merges. Hence it is said:

> Mere *suffering exists, no sufferer is found; the deed is,*
> *but no doer of the deed is there; nibbāna is, but not the*
> *man who enters it; the path is, but no traveller on it*
> *is seen.*   (**Visuddhimagga** XVI)

Even the above quotation is beyond the grasping of ordinary "worldlings". Hence they are only taught to practice the two *pāramitās* : *dāna* and *sila*. With generosity and morality as a basis, one could be happy in a worldly way and even expect a heavenly reward after death (*sagga*). This is regarded as a skillful way of teaching to most people. Those who are dissatisfied with worldly happiness (*kāmadīnava*) then need renunciation (*nekkhamma*) in order to perfect morality, as one is still a householder during the first stage of morality. As a householder, one has to exploit others through one's profession or family. Even within the family itself, there is plenty of room for exploitation, knowingly or unknowingly.

Unfortunately, in the Theravāda tradition, only those who leave home for the homeless life of almsmen and almswomen would be in a position to understand the Four Noble Truths and the doctrine of Dependent Origination.

Despite the fact that Anatha Pindika was very generous with gifts to the *sangha* and to the needy, and he had also strictly adhered to the ethical code for laymen, he was not taught the Ultimate Truth of reality until he was dying. It was considered unskillful to cling to life, property and family.

A skillful teacher shows householders how to behave between friends, children and parents, teachers and pupils, employers and employees, husband and wife, as well as teaching the duties connected with means of livelihood and the layman's relation to the state.

Both householders and those who leave home for the homeless life are skillfully taught to be aware of worldly conditions (*loka-dhamma*), since "they arise in connection with worldly life—gain and loss, honor and dishonor, happiness and misery, praise and blame." One should be aware of them and not be attached to them.

Only the one who trains himself/herself beyond the 'mundane' (*lokiya*), "through the extinction of all cankers (*āsava-kkhaya*)... reaches immediately in this very life the deliverance of mind, the deliverance through wisdom which is free from cankers and which he/she has understood and realized."

Only then, could the term *nibbāna* as Unborn, Unoriginated, Uncreated, Unformed be understood as "the unfading, the undecaying, the unaging, the undying, the taintless, the deathless, the secure, the goal." Ordinary human experience could never render the ultimate state of the supramundane. *nibbānic* experience is beyond the mundane state of theoretical formulation. However, in ordinary language, *nibbāna* is 'inner freedom, equilibrium, peace, void of angst and a sense of being entirely 'at home' and unthreatened in the universe, which expresses itself both in a positive, effective state and as compassion for all forms of life.' These marvellous words are still inadequate to express *nibbāna*. One could even put it bluntly as "the permanent, immortal, supramundane state which cannot be expressed in mundane terms."

With the above approach to understanding ultimate reality in the Theravāda tradition, I feel that if our Christian friends would extrapolate Christ's teachings on love and morality as expressed in the parable of the Good Samaritan and the Sermon on the Mount, we would have a lot in common. If the Church would skillfully relate morality to the absolute, as in the case of divorce, abortion, birth control and family planning, people would be free to pursue their own livelihood, rather than being told what is right and wrong as if they were children.

Church leaders should be good friends (*kalayānamitta*) to members of their congregation, wishing their welfare and concerned with their progress. If church leaders have developed spiritually, they could be the voice of conscience (*paratoghosa*) to help the faithful to tread the path towards God.

By developing skillful means, it does not mean that Christians are not to believe in God, but that their confidence in absolute reality is similar to the Buddhists. For Theravādins, the Buddha is the noted example of the one who has achieved all the ten perfections. But to understand him fully or to see him, one has to reach the ultimate end of suffering, or understand the doctrine of Dependent Origination so clearly that one has the Dhamma-Eye. Hence, one who sees the Dhamma, sees the Buddha. It is stated in Mahāyāna that the ultimate Dharmakāyā is "eternal, unalterable, indestructible, unchangeable, constant, everlasting, imperishable."

Likewise, those who could see God are not dogmatic theologians but mystics like Meister Eckhart who make a distinction between *deus*, the personal God, and *deitas*, the Godhead, of which God is a manifestation to humankind. One can liken *nibbāna* to the transpersonal Godhead.

Edward Conze said, "When we compare the essential attributes of the Godhead as they are understood by the more mystical traditions of Christian thought with those of nirvana, we find almost no difference at all. It is assumed first of all that there is an ultimate reality, and secondly that there is a point in ourselves at which we touch that ultimate reality. The ultimate reality, also called dhamma by the Buddhists, or *nibbāna*, is defined as that which stands completely outside the sensory world of illusion and ignorance, a world inextricably interwoven with craving and greed. To get somehow to that ultimate reality is the supremely worthwhile goal of the Buddhist life. The Buddhist idea of ultimate reality is very much akin to the philosophical notion of the 'Absolute' and not easily distinguished from the notion of God among more mystical theologians, like Dionysius Aeropagita and Eckhart". (quoted in John Hick, "Religion as skillful means: a hint from Buddhism").

From a Buddhist perspective, if we could use skillful means to define God undogmatically, and encourage that understanding amongst the faithful, Christian ethics would become more positive to Christians and non-Christians alike. As Hick says, "there is no such thing as the universally agreed Christian understanding of God, Christ, redemption, humanity, the church and its priesthood, of the nature of theology, or the things to come. Christian interpretations of all these main themes vary from one historical epoch to another, and in a given epoch from one region to another, and within a given region, from one group to another, and within a given group often even from one individual to another."

According to Buddhism, all of these manifestations of ultimate reality are modes of *upāya*. They are ways in which particular faiths (formed by their own traditions) communicate, conceive and experience the ultimate in relation to themselves. Hence, they cannot demand that others agree with them.

The notion of *upāya* is the notion that the cosmic significance of the *nibbanic* experience can be conceptualized in a variety of ways, all of which communicate the importance and availability of a particular experience, but none that constitute the only correct way of conceptualizing it. These schemes of thought are provisional and instrumental and are to be discarded like the raft that has fulfilled its function in the Buddha's parable.

This means that the Buddhist notion of the absolute is more careful and it implies the tolerance of other views, including those of folk beliefs, shamanism, magic-religious teachings, or other religions and philosophies that express entries into truth.

However, if one carries the notion of skillful means too far, it seems that trickery and falsehood are permitted if helping others is achieved. Again, the Buddhist middle way can be used not to tread on a slippery path.

I agree with David Lochhead that 'our language can only convey a likeness, an imitation of the reality of God, which is expressed to our finite imagination.' Hopefully, what I have said so far may be somewhat useful to our Buddhist-Christian dialogues. I will not comment on the excellent paper on "Christian Upāya: Variations on a theme by Soren Kierkegard". I will only mention the 'two truths'—conventional and ultimate.

The Buddha, in explaining his doctrine, sometimes used conventional language and sometimes a more philosophical mode of expression which is in accord with undeluded insight into reality.

Ultimately, existence is a mere process of physical and mental phenomena within which, or beyond which, no real ego-entity nor any abiding substance can be found. Thus, whenever the *suttas* speak of man, woman, or person, or of the rebirth of a being, this must not be taken as being valid in the ultimate sense, but as a mere conventional mode of speech. Those statements of the Buddha couched in conventional language are also called 'truth' (*vohāra-sacca*), being relatively correct, which does not contradict the fact that such statements ultimately refer to impermanent and impersonal processes.

The two truths—ultimate and conventional—appear in that form only in the commentaries, but are implied in a *sutta* distinction of "explicit (or direct) meaning (*nitattha*) and an implicit meaning (to be inferred) (*neyyattha*). Further, the Buddha repeatedly mentioned his reservations when using conventional speech, for example, "Those are merely names, expression, terms of speech, designations in common use in the world, which the *Tathagata* uses without misapprehending them."

Bhikkhu Buddhadāsa developed the Buddha's method into two kinds of language: Dhammic (*Bhāsā-Dham*) and humanly (*Bhāsā-Khon*).

He reminds his followers that when they read the Buddhist scriptures about heavenly and hellish realms, they must interpret them beyond the usual worldly meaning, to see whether or not such a passage leads them "to welfare, truths, or the leading of the Higher life, to disenchantment (with the world), to the absence of desire, to calm, to thorough understanding, to the Highest Wisdom, or to the Final of *nibbāna*."

The same applies to the Buddhist understanding of Christian terms such as salvation, Holy Spirit, Christ, Non-being, or phrases such as "a conscious recommitment to God made real to apostles by Jesus", "Freedom from self-concern, based on trust in God", and the concept of Christian saints as the centrality of the divine in human lives.

Once one can go beyond the concept of egoism, one will understand that the Christians use worldly language to express the ultimate truth, and that fundamental to this cosmic confidence is the radical transcendence of ego.

Bearing this in mind, the Buddhists will understand Paul's utterance to be similar in dhammic language in their own tradition. When he said, "I live, and yet not I, but Christ lives in me...", the Christian meanings of love, joy, peace and temperance become meaningful to Buddhists. Buddhadāsa even goes further in telling his followers to look at the cross as a symbol which signifies the abolition of "I".

II

My response to Lochhead's Christian *upāya* from a Theravada perspective has come to a similar conclusion, that we both need social transformation in addition to individual transformation from a selfish to a selfless being.

I am attracted by Christian liberation theology, especially in Latin America. I regret that none of them is on our International Buddhist-Christian Theological Encounter Group. From my reading of Paul F Knitter, Raimundo Panikkar, Leonardo Boff and Jon Sobrino, I have come to appreciate the subjects of liberation theology.

The suffering people of Latin America use liberation theology to free themselves from the oppressive system there as Minchuang theology in South Korea. In their Buddhist counterpart of former South Vietnam, Thich Nhat Hanh and his Tiep Hien order also produced a unique expression of traditional morality to come to terms with contemporary issues. These precepts were not developed by secluded monks attempting to update traditional Buddhism; they were forged in the crucible of war and devastation that was the daily experience for many Southeast Asians during the past several decades.

This means that the dogmatic or scriptural formations of the past, though remaining normative, are not absolute norms. The "truth" of dogma and tradition must be constantly exposed to the 'ultimate arbitor' of truth—that is, the transformative response to

Christian praxis "right knowing" (orthodoxy) without "right doing" (orthopraxis) cannot exist. This means that orthodoxy must be adjusted under the pressure of orthopraxis and that one can bear with uncertainty what is orthodoxy as long as one is able to responsibly bring about transformation and liberation in the world. The primacy of praxis also sets up a defence system against the persistent danger of the decay of doctrine into ideology. By submitting their cherished beliefs to the test of praxis, Christians are better able to recognize how much such belief—for example, in Christ—is possibly nurtured more by the desire to maintain power and privilege than by the desire to promote truth and freedom. In unmasking ideology and in submitting orthodoxy to the constant criticism of orthopraxis, liberation theologians clear the ground for a more fertile dialogue.

Not only is the ground for dialogue cleared, but an effective launching pad is provided. To begin—and to maintain—dialogue, it is not necessary that all parties agree on certain universal truths, for instance, if there is one incarnate or many. The mutual starting point will be how Christians and others can struggle together against those that threaten their common humanity, for example, consumerism (greed), militarism (hatred) and the destruction of the environment (delusion). Only in the praxis of such struggle can clarity of universal truths emerge.

Indeed, liberation Christology allows and may require that Christians recognize the possibility of other saviors or incarnations. If a liberation praxis is the foundation for the authentic revelation of truth, then Christians can open to the possibility that other religious visions will offer a liberating praxis and promise a kingdom equal to that of Jesus. In view of their fruits of praxis, such saviours would have to be recognized and affirmed. Again, their existence would in no way have to jeopardize the universal relevance of Jesus's vision or lessen one's total commitment to it.

For those of us who regularly attend the International Buddhist-Christian Theological Encounter, the above statement may be acceptable. But our last meeting was at the Chinese Buddhist temple near Los Angeles and a Thai-Christian in the area told me that she would never go to a place of the devil! In fact many Christians will feel their faith threatened by the suggestion that Jesus may or may not be God's definitive revelation, or that there may be other saviors and other incarnations.

A Christian friend suggested that the feeling of being threatened by 'other saviors' arises not from the spontaneous voice of faith but from unquestioned presuppositions. The Western philosophical notion that for something to be really true and worthy of their commitment it must be the only truth has given rise to this kind of blind belief.

Again, what I have said earlier on *upāya*, the ultimate and conventional language, may be helpful to those who wish to go beyond the call of orthodoxy.

Religious people must recognize that religion itself has no permanent form or expression. The basic principles may be un-changing, but the forms and practices evolve. In teaching Buddhism in the West, for example, a Tibetan should not establish Buddhism exactly as it existed in Tibet because the conditions here are different. This does not mean that culture needs to be rejected, but it should carefully be distinguished from religion. Likewise, if the Christians wish to preserve their own European cultural heritage, they must be mindful that each culture has both strengths and weaknesses. They should not expect others—Asians, Africans, Latin Americans—who want to practice Christianity to adopt the exploitive and aggressive characteristic of culture.

As Ashish Nandi explained clearly in his book, **The Intimate Enemy**, Gandhi appealed to the basic teaching of Christ on truth, love and non-violence so that his movement would be supported by the British who felt that they should practice Christianity—as the religion of the oppressed and not the oppressors.

The greatest obstacle to the flowering of universal love—the core of all faith—is the relationship between religion and culture. Religion usually has a significant influence on culture, but when we mistake culture for religion, the result is usually sectarianism. The tribal element, with its potential for chauvinism and violence begins to dominate. Even the Christian God could be the angry God of the Selected, who were the Jews and later the British and now the Americans!

Over the past two centuries, in all the world's religions, universal love has become secondary to outer forms, so that purely institutionalized religions are the norm. Most churches support the political status quo no matter how oppressive the ruling regimes may be. Their religious hierarchies have become entrenched and their vision static. Since the rise of capitalism, all of the world's great faiths have catered to the rich, even if their leaders pay lip service to the poor. There have not been enough prophetic voices to keep the social and economic order moving towards peace and justice for all of humankind.

In the 18th century, priestly power began to decline and a new kind of mentor, the secular intellectual captured the ear of society. In their earliest incarnations as priests, scribes, soothsayers, and intellectuals they have always guided us, but their insights were limited by the canons of tradition. They were not free spirits or adventurers of consciousness.

Today, these secularists are not bound by tradition but rise up and claim that they can diagnose and cure all of our society's ills with their intellects. They even claim that they can devise formulas that will change not only the structure of society but the fundamental habits of human beings. Unlike their sacerdotal predecessors, they are merely substitute servants and interpreters of the gods. Their hero is Prometheus, who stole the celestial fire and brought it to Earth.

One of the characteristics of the new secular intellectuals is their eagerness to scrutinize religion and its protagonists. These intellectuals examine how far the great systems of faith have aided or harmed humanity and to what extent religious leaders have lived up to their precept of purity, truthfulness, charity and benevolence. Then they issue harsh pronouncements against both churches and clergy.

Unfortunately these secular gods failed because, like their priestly predecessors, they became arrogant and intolerant. In many cases, ideas and the direction of humanity became more important to them than the individuals they encountered. Most of them lacked commitment to personal transformation.

We have more than enough programs, organizations, parties and strategies in the world for the alleviation of suffering and injustice. In fact, we place too much faith in the power of action, especially political action. This leads to social activism preoccupying itself with external conditions.

Like the secular intellectuals, activists tend to see all malevolence as being caused by the "system" without understanding how negative factors also operate within ourselves. They approach global problems with the mentality of social engineering, assuming that personal virtue will result from a radical restructuring of society.

The opposite view that radical transformation of society requires personal and spiritual change first or at least simultaneously—has been accepted by Buddhists and many other religious adherents. Hopefully, liberation Christians also recognize the importance of personal transformation. Those who want to change society must understand the inner dimension of change. It is this sense of personal transformation that religion can provide. Simply performing the outer rituals of any tradition has little value if it is not accompanied by inner personal transformation. Religious values are those that give voice to the spiritual depths of humanity. There are many descriptions of the religious experience but all relate to becoming less and less selfish.

As this transformation is achieved, we also require a greater moral responsibility. Spiritual considerations and social change are seen to be inseparable. Forces in our social environment such as consumerism, with its emphasis on craving and dissatisfaction, can hinder our spiritual development.

People seeking to live spiritually must be concerned with their social and physical environment. To be truly religious is not to reject society but to work for social justice and change. Religious Buddhism or Christianity is at the heart of social justice and change and social change is the essence of religion.

[A paper prepared for the 4th International Buddhist-Christian Conference, "Buddhism, Christianity & Global Healing" at Boston University, 30 July - 5 August 1992.]

APPLYING GANDHI FOR
ALTERNATIVE TO CONSUMERISM

I

It is with no false modesty that I feel unworthy of the great honor of having been invited to deliver the Annual Gandhi Peace Foundation Lecture on the 50th anniversary of the Mahatma's martyrdom. I will try my utmost to demonstrate that his examples and vision can be very appropriately applied today in overcoming globalization and establishing an alternative to consumerism.

I think Vandana Shiva was right when she said colonialism, development and globalization are synonymous, although they have consequences of differing levels of severity.

The colonial masters were very skillful in creating the image of empire as a valuable system, whereby the Europeans had the right to rule other parts of the world for the benefit of the natives, who could not run their own countries or maintain justice and peace. It was the so-called aristocrats of Europe, or those who aspired to the upper classes, who accepted the "burden" of providing, outside of their countries, western administration, education and technology for various parts of the empire, so that the natives would be "civilized" in the European sense of the word. As Disraeli said, the East is a career. In the case of the British Empire, all natives were treated as British subjects, and English training was provided for those fortunate enough to have access to education. The clever men—never the women—could even study Latin and Greek. The Indian Civil Service (ICS) was created as a system of education and administration so that the British subjects could feel superior to the non ICS. On top of that, the privileged natives could even go to Britain, to enter public schools, and for further education at Oxbridge, or to be called to the Bar, in order to become "English gentlemen" at heart, despite their brown or black appearances.

Both Gandhi and Nehru were no doubt greatly influenced by their British education. Had Gandhi not been shocked by the rough, ungentlemanly treatment by the Whites in South Africa, his faith in the British Empire might never have really been shaken. I am afraid Nehru never received this kind of psychological shock, despite the fact that he fought for Indian independence and was imprisoned many times. As a result, he ran independent India similar to the manner in which his English contemporaries from Cambridge ran the British Empire—with a sense of fairness to his beloved Indians yet remaining an aristocrat, establishing perhaps unintentionally a dynasty of three generations, insisting on centralization and the advancement of technology, with democracy along the lines of Westminster, leaning towards the ideology of the Labour Party. Nehru's role in the non-aligned world could really be seen as that of head of another empire, or another commonwealth, with Nehru as the uncrowned monarch.

Had Nehru followed in Gandhi's footsteps, in the latter's concepts of decentralization in the form of village republics and of an alternative to western civilization and technology, India would really have been a shining example in today's world, especially as the established eurocentric forms of capitalistic economics and politics, and education as well, have come to real catastrophe.

One might well be justified in claiming that the beginning of the decline and fall of the British Empire began with the "Swadeshi" movement started by Gandhi, especially after the Salt March in 1930. India's Independence in 1947 made "colonialism" a dirty word, even for some Labour leaders in London. When Truman became President of the US, in his inaugural speech on January 20th, 1949 he clearly stated that the word 'development' must replace the word 'colonialism' meaning that the white man didn't need to occupy land overseas anymore, but rather needed to use psychological warfare to brainwash the natives, especially the leaders of the newly independent countries, to feel "underdeveloped". To this end they should be brought to join Free Trade (which is not fair trade) and free democracy in the American fashion; meaning that if right-wing dictators follow American Free Trade and became junior partners of the US, they were "democratic" and on the road to development. This was the case with Thailand, Pakistan, South Korea and the former South Vietnam.

In the case of Thailand, the use of the old name, Siam, signifies something old fashioned and "underdeveloped" although not by shaking off the vestiges of a past colonial power, as Siam was never colonized—not politically at any rate. Buddhism teaches the people to be content and to live simply, in villages, surrounded by nature; our people did this, and related to each other fraternally, almost equally, with the common ultimate goal of liberation from greed, hatred and delusion. The name of the country had to be changed, as a symbolic gesture of a departure from these past principles, to Thailand—an anglicized hybrid word, symbolizing the country's desire to embrace the process of development or westernization in the American image. American "experts" told the Thai government that Buddhism was unhealthy to the process of development, as it does not encourage competition, nor the accumulation of wealth, and it is also atheist. As a result Buddhism was encouraged to limit its role to private spirituality for the individual and mere ceremony for the masses. Its teachings in the social and political spheres were curtailed; instead, the government used propaganda to brainwash the people to make money, at any cost, by right or wrong livelihood. The more the Thai government followed the development pattern set out by the American "experts", by building more roads, more dams, by producing more electricity and television sets, the more the gap between the rich and the poor in the country widened, and the more the natural environment was destroyed. The American presence in Siam during the Vietnam war made Bangkok and Pataya notorious as centres for sex tourism and the like; this is just an example of the consequences of development in the American image. Another result is that Bangkok, once a beautiful capital city, has become heavily polluted, blocked by traffic jams, full of slums, and so is now very ugly. The villages, too, have largely been destroyed; the young have all left to seek employment in the city, or abroad.

The Americans introduced the "Decades of Development" to the UN in the 1960s and 1970s; as a result, many refer to these years as the Decades of Shame. Because of this, the American neo-colonialism in the name of development is on the decline. The transnational corporations are now our new masters; they rule the world, as David Korten rightly says. They use the media to manipulate people into being merely their employees or consumers of their unnecessary products; they create a sense of lack in people, who no longer interact, nor live in natural surrounding, but instead are conditioned to their meaningless jobs, just to be paid; conditioned by television boxes or computer screens to live in the unreal world of consumerism.

It is not too late, however, to look back to Gandhi and learn from him, from his thoughts, his works, his action, and his lifestyle. I think this could contribute positively, not only to the battle against colonialism, and neo-colonialism in the name of national development, but also to the creation of alternative societies against globalization and its demonic religion or ideology, consumerism.

II

Ashish Nandi stated clearly in *The Intimate Enemy* that Gandhi's victory over the British Empire was due largely to the extent to which his genuine spiritual and moral commitment appealed to the hearts and pricked the conscience of religious leaders in the West, with their ideal that one should serve the universal God of truth, sacrifice, love, compassion and equality, and not the tribal God of the empire, where the white men had special privilege over the natives.

Indeed, Gandhi was able to apply the best of Hinduism, Buddhism and Christianity to his lifestyle and his movement with *satyagraha* and *ahimsa*. His genuine respect for Islam and Sikhism, as well, was so profound that he was endeared to all those seeking the essence of any spiritual tradition.

J.L. Mehta puts it more beautifully, that through Gandhi, the Indian can joyfully let his religious imagination be enlarged and vivified by the heritage of the Greeks, by the vision of Christianity, and the message of Islam, and he can freely seek to appreciate through creative reinterpretation the tradition of which he is both a product and a trustee. He can accomplish this, but only to the extent that he can see himself and his tradition in the wider inter-religious context of world history, (quoted by Fred Dallmayr in *Beyond Orientalism*, SUNY Press, Albany 1996, p.114).

This reminds me of my own Siamese teacher, the late Venerable Bhikkhu Buddhadasa, who taught that: 1) We should understand and practice what is best in our own religion;   2) We should sincerely respect our friends' religions; and 3) We should all unite to fight non-violently against greed, hatred and delusion, which can now be seen as personified by materialism, consumerism and egotism.

Gandhi certainly fulfilled all three of these teachings, and did not make a distinction between spirituality and morality on the one hand and politics and economics on the other, but rather treated them all as inter-related.

> "True economics never militates against the highest ethical standard, just as all true ethics to be worth its name must, at the same time, be also good economics. An economics that inculcates Mammon worship, and enables the strong to amass wealth at the expense of the weak, is a false and dismal science. It spells death. True economics on the other hand, stands for social justice, it promotes the good of all equally, including the weakest, and is indispensable for decent life."

This quotation would have no real meaning if it did not come from a man who lived these words. For me, Gandhi's words, like the Buddha, link directly with his thoughts, his actions and his lifestyle. His deep spiritual commitment to the transformation of his personality from selfishness to ever greater selflessness was vital to his achievement, personally, culturally, socially, politically and economically.

Satish Kumar rightly maintains that Gandhi felt that, to create a new way of life or restore the proper way of life, we need three elements—vision, nonviolent resistance and alternative practice.

Without vision, meaning is lost. Contemporary intellectuals often lack this depth of vision; besides, intellectuals are now so secular and profane that their moral behaviour is usually dubious —some are even violent. Intellectuals are good at analyzing what is wrong, and how we can put it right—usually by social engineering: intellectuals or technocrats only use their heads, not their hearts, to solve problems.

For Gandhi, however, a deep ocean of vision and values was essential, to build a new way of life, which must be rooted in culture and civilization, in local wisdom, and in a spiritual environment.

Rabindranath Tagore echoes this sentiment when he says

"Contemporary Western civilization is built of brick and wood. It is rooted in the city. But Indian civilization has been distinctive in locating its source of regeneration, material and intellectual, in the forest, not the city. India's best ideas have come where people were in communion with trees and rivers and lakes, away from the crowds. The culture of the forest has fueled the culture of Indian society—the culture that has arisen from the forest has been influenced by the diverse processes of renewal of life which are always at play in the forest, varying from species to species, from season to season, in sight and sound and smell. The unifying principle of life in diversity, of democratic pluralism, thus became the principle of Indian civilization."

It was on this distinctiveness that Mahatma Gandhi built his ideas and actions for freedom and democracy. The faulty logic of resource exploitation, integral to the classical model of economic development based on resource-intensive technologies, led Gandhi to seek an alternative path of development for India. He wrote: "God forbid that India should ever take to industrialism after the manner of the West. The economic imperialism of a single tiny island kingdom (England) is today keeping the world in chains. If an entire nation of 300 million took to similar economic exploitation, it would strip the world bare like locusts."

If we miss this vital difference, the east will follow the west blindly. Luckily, quite a number of western thinkers have now begun to look seriously to the east, as western civilization and city have been cut off from their roots for so long, specifically since the age of enlightenment and the so-called modernization.

For example, Maurice Ash, son-in-law of Leonard Elmhirst who was once Secretary to Tagore, calls in question the west's trail of flawed knowledges, of which a hopeless search for God is characteristic. If we are to step back from the brink of environmental catastrophes, we must attempt the re-empowerment of the local, or the village republics, so to speak. Only thus could interconnectedness be restored as a prevailing characteristic of our lives; only thus could there really be a positive future. This is the same as the essence of Buddhist teaching, as seen in the law of interdependent origination, which can be applied to society.

Had Prince Siddhartha remained in the palace, in the city, there would be no Buddhism; indeed the Buddha was born under a tree, was awakened under a tree, preached his first sermon in the grove, and called his monasteries "groves". He spent most of his time underneath trees, in the groves or in the forest; he even passed away under twin trees.

Buddhist teachings provide a means of evaluating the nature and direction of global development. The approach is significant in that it entails a consideration of the extent to which social and economic policies tend to contribute to or diminish human suffering. This aspect is often obscured by the quest for modernization and westernization.

Had Gandhi remained in the city, he would have remained an urban intellectual, like many of his contemporaries. He went out to the poor, to live in the villages, to establish ashrams as alternatives. This is what provided the deep ocean of vision and values which was essential in order to build a new way of life for the mutltitude.

In this desire for a new way of life, an alternative to the prevailing one, Gandhi resisted the status quo. He not only denounced imported British clothes, but called upon people to bring out all their British-made clothes and burn them. This was resistance against the global, exploitative economics of the British empire. He also boycotted English education, which was brainwashing the natives to admire the British establishment, and teaching them to become clerks or employees, to respect their superiors, without any spiritual dimension or critical awareness of the unjust structural violence of the empire.

While resisting the most powerful empire of the day, Gandhi also started constructive programs for his people. Not only should people burn British clothes, he said, but they should start using the spinning wheel, to make their own khadi. Not only should people refuse British education, but he provided alternative schooling for them, as well as alternative food and medicine. Indeed, the spinning wheel became the symbol of home economics and home rule.

It required genius to reduce things to this degree of simplicity, practicality and straight-forwardness. Spinning your own clothes meant alternative economics of self-reliance, for every household and every village.

Had he lived longer his dream might have been fulfilled —his village republics might have become a reality: "In this structure composed of innumerable villages, there will be ever-widening, never ascending circles. Life will not be a pyramid with the apex sustained by the bottom. It will be an oceanic circle whose center will be the individual always ready to perish for the village, the village ready to perish for the circle of villages till at last the whole becomes one life composed of individuals, never aggressive in their arrogance, but ever humble, sharing the majesty of the oceanic circle of which they are an integral part."

Mr. Pridi Banomyong introduced constitutional monarchy to Siam in 1932, with a vision of nonviolence and righteousness; he also founded the Dharmashastra University in 1934 to teach the young to have the moral courage to serve politics as free citizens, bounded by fraternity, equality and liberty (though not in the western sense of the words). He tried to destroy centralization, colonial administration and hierarchy by going back to the root of *sangha*, or Buddhist democracy. Unfortunately, he was pushed out of power by the military in 1947. We hope to bring his concept of Dharmic Socialism—not Statism as in the former USSR—back to the country and the region by the year 2000, his centenary. By combining Pridi's Dharmic Society with Gandhi's vital elements of spiritual commitment, clear vision, nonviolent resistance, and constructive program, we could really create a powerful movement against global economics, megatechnology and the transnational corporations, with their demonic religion or ideology, consumerism.

III

When the Soviet Union was established in 1918, many left wing intellectuals thought this was a chance for an alternative to capitalism; yet George Orwell maintained sixty years ago that the USSR would collapse, and though no one believed him, this became true in 1992. Orwell had contended that any nation state which has no moral legitimacy to rule its people cannot endure. It was for this reason that the British empire collapsed, due largely to public conscientization by Gandhi for an alternative lifestyle, despite the fact that many British imperialists claimed that their government promoted fairness, the rule of law, and the advantages of an English education.

They justified imperialism using racism, on the grounds that the indigenous people could not rule themselves properly or fairly. Churchill recalls the confidence of Britons who "thought they could

teach the world the art of government, and the science of economics."
The British empire used education and colonial administration, as well as the judicial system, to mask their ulterior motive of oppression and capitalistic exploitation. We are now confronted with a new form of empire, configured by the transnational corporations. This empire is dependent upon the media to disguise its true purpose, and to promote the fiction that development is good and that globalization is beneficial to all, which is in fact, a lie.

The G-7 group of industrialized countries, which has now enlarged to eight, is not itself a new empire, but rather a rich man's club and an oppressor's club, which is designed to serve the interests of the transnational corporations. The mainstream media are instruments of their policies, and are effectively manipulated by the corporate interests. It is very clear how the media are captivated by luxurious or violent events and led to focus on the top politicians, who serve the rich and the powerful.

David Korten was right when he entitled his book, **When Corporations Rule the World**, and Bishop Desmond Tutu rightly said about the book, that it is a "searing indictment of an unjust international economic order." Yet the big industrialized countries are supporting this unjust economic order, as their leaders support the World Bank, the International Monetary Fund, and the World Trade Organization. These are linked to the transnational corporations, and together they harm our environment, our mother Earth, and our people—not only the indigenous peoples and other poor people in the South, but even the labourers and the middle classes in the North are being increasingly exploited.

In Kirkpatrick Sales' book about the Luddites, **Rebel Against the Future**, he says that the industrial revolution in England during the last century destroyed the British farmers for the benefit of the landlords and industrialists, for the growth of capitalism and the expansion of the empire; not to mention the fact that craftsmen were forced to become labourers. He says that the new empire of globalization, run by the transnational corporations and their megatechnology and computers, will make most members of the middle classes jobless within two decades.

However, I can see no sign of the G-7 confronting this dilemma. Russia was invited to join the club not because it is rich economically, but because it is rich in natural resources. With the elimination of the communist or socialist ideology as opposition to the capitalist ideology of transnational corporations, globalization will allow the transnationals to plunder more of these natural resources.

The consequences of this destruction of the environment will first be felt by the indigenous peoples, in the form of the destruction of their livelihood and dignity. The middle class will also ultimately face destruction in deference to the profit motive, a further sacrifice at the altar of money and technology.

Globalization is indeed a new demonic religion. It uses the media to create a sense of lack; hence we are driven to earn more in order to acquire more, yet can never reach a point of contentment. Since the process of globalization is under the control of the big corporations, the media is used to direct us blindly towards the monoculture of ever-increasing technology, of the McWorld of fast food and junk food, and of the "cola and jeans" syndrome.

But if we emulate the American and the G-7 lifestyles, there will not be sufficient natural resources for all of us. Most of us will not be happy with this mode of life, which is harmful to ourselves, our family, our society and our natural environment. If, however, we follow the way of the indigenous peoples, we can all live simply and have time to enjoy ourselves and be part and parcel of the community, as well as of our mother earth.

We should also learn from Gandhi, especially his deep spiritual commitment to truth, *satyagraha*, his deep vision, nonviolent resistance, and practice of an alternative lifestyle. In this way, we would achieve wholeness of life, and maintain the sanctity of the natural order.

We should learn to be alone with nature, to live with birds and deer, to appreciate nature and respect nature. Only then can we realize that intellectualism and social engineering cannot liberate us from suffering.

We need to return to the best of our spiritual tradition, to shamanism, to mythology, to traditional rituals, songs and dances, to experience life as it is still alive and available in many indigenous communities which are being threatened by big corporate entities, which are supported by states in the G-7 and others, in derogation of the interests of their own people and natural resources.

For the corporations, natural resources are only a source of economic gain; when one area has been exhausted, they will move on to another. The people are relevant only to the extent that they serve to generate income, either as laborers or consumers. For spiritual people and those who follow the essence of Gandhi's teaching, money is less important; of greater significance, for them and for us, is to be self-reliant; to have home economics; to live happily, with dignity, with a sense of the sacred, with a spiritual dimension to our lives, and in harmony with the earth; with reverence for our ancestors, respect for our communities, and with a commitment to the generations to come.

If we care for our survival, we must not only question the G-7 economic policies, but also the political structure that has emerged, and which is no longer accountable to the people, as well as the legal and judicial systems which serve to maintain the status quo.

Thich Nhat Hanh reminds us not to avoid contact with suffering or close our eyes before suffering; not to lose awareness of the existence of suffering in the life of the world; to find a way to be with those who are suffering, using all means at our disposal, including personal contact and visits, images, sounds, by such means to awaken ourselves and others to the reality of suffering in the world.

Nhat Hanh tells us further that we should not lose ourselves in dispersion and in our surroundings; that we should practice mindful breathing to come back to what is happening in the present moment, to be in touch with what is wondrous, refreshing and healing, both inside and around us; that we should plant seeds of joy, peace and understanding in ourselves, in order to facilitate the work of transformation in the depths of our consciousness.

We need alternative economic and political strategies designed as if human beings matter. We need alternative educational programs which encourage us to integrate the manifold aspects of our being. We must be able to link our head with our heart, so that we can escape compartmentalization and develop the capacity to grow seeds of peace and seeds of joy within ourselves. And from this, we can bring about change; not by hating the oppressor, but by challenging the structural violence. Through nonviolent means, we can seek a transformation to a just and peaceful world.

Science used to stand in opposition to the established religion. Indeed, Scientism was subconsciously manipulated by many western scientists in the name of objective experiments and observation, in search for knowledge, which was materialistic, compartmental and unethical. But there is now a new scientific approach to the living universe, which produces a new kind of scientist, who is humble and relies upon the heart as well as the head. This science links beautifully with the best in spiritual endeavour, and can help us to appreciate the wholeness of being. I hope that we are together in this venture. By learning from Gandhi and applying his examples appropriately we can have a new movement against globalization by the transnational corporations, and towards reliance on local culture and communities. This is essential if we are to live happily together, with wisdom, understanding, and love.

[Lecture delivered by Sulak Sivaraksa on January 30 1998, the 50th death anniversary of Mahatma Gandhi at the Gandhi Peace Foundation, New Delhi. It was published in *Gandhi Marg* Vol.15 No.4 January - March 1998.]

PART II

UNPO

HUMAN RIGHTS AWARD

1998

Mr Sulak Sivaraksa

*For recognition of service
to unrepresented nations and
peoples and for the adherence
to the principles and ideals
enshrined in the UNPO Covenant.*

THE 1998 UNPO AWARD

The Hague, July 28, 1998

Dear Mr Sulak Sivraksa,

On behalf of the first Awards Committee of the **Unrepresented Nations and People Organisation** it gives me great pleasure to announce that you have been chosen to receive one of two of the 1998 UNPO-Awards. You were selected from a large number of nominees.

You have been chosen for your deep commitment to peace and non-violence as well as for your courageous leadership and inspiration to others. You have over the years been an articulate and daring voice of peace, human rights and social justice, not only in your native Thailand, where you have been for forty years an outspoken advocate for democracy, but also in the international arena.

You embody the spirit in which UNPO was created; the spirit of co-operation, of sharing, yet with respect for the differences, and empathy for their problems. You are a source of inspiration, motivation and solidarity to everyone who believes in democracy, human rights and self-determination.

The other award winner is Buddhist Master Cheng Yen of Taiwan for her devoted efforts over many decades that have touched the lives in poor and disaster stricken areas in many countries all over the world.

Therefore, UNPO would be very honoured to present to you the UNPO-Award during the eighteenth Steering Committee Meeting that will be held in Taipei, Taiwan through 23-26 of September 1998.

Yours sincerely,

Ms. Helen Corbett
General Secretary

ACCEPTANCE SPEECH

It is indeed a great honor and privilege for me to receive the UNPO award here in Taiwan. I feel very humbled, especially to know that my fellow recipient is the Venerable Cheng Yen. She is a renown humanitarian whose charity and generosity has touched innumerable lives in impoverished and disaster stricken areas throughout the world. In comparison, my contribution is like a speck of dust.

In 1995, when I was awarded by the Right Livelihood Foundation in Sweden, I had just won a case on defaming the King in my country which was brought against me by the army commander-in-chief. Cases like this usually ended up with conviction with a maximum penalty of 15 years imprisonment. I fought the case for 4 years. Thanks to my lawyers, as well as local and international supporters, I won the case—a rare phenomenon in Thai history.

While receiving the UNPO award, I am again a defendant on yet another criminal case for obstructing the gas-pipeline from Burma to Siam. The pipeline was built by two multinational Oil Corporations, Unocal in the US and Total in France in collaboration with the Thai government and the Burmese military junta. In building this pipeline, many ethnic minorities in Burma suffer tremendously, forests have been destroyed, and the Thai people are disturbed—not to mention the effects on wildlife. I am now on bail and will return to fight the case in court on 27th October and 3rd November. I hope to ask the court to tell the public how wicked multinational corporations are, especially when they work with dictatorial regimes like the one in Burma which uses investment in oil companies to launder drug money and to purchase arms to kill various ethnic peoples. I may also be charged again with another case of defaming the king. If so, this will be the third time in my life.

When the United Nations was founded over half a century ago, the preamble started with 'we the people' who agreed together to prevent war, to uphold human dignity and human rights. Unfortunately, the UN has become a very prestigious international organization, which represents only governments. As we know, most governments do not represent the people, especially ethnic minorities and the poor. Most governments, knowingly or unknowingly, serve multinational corporations, the International Monetary Fund, the World Bank and the World Trade Organization. I am very glad therefore that there is such an international organization like the UNPO—for the Underrepresented Nations and Peoples. I believe Taiwan is also a member of the UNPO, as is Tibet, East Timor, Mon, Hawaii and other indigenous peoples. For those who want their nations to be free from occupation and oppression, the UNPO works nonviolently and lawfully within their own territories as well as international and this makes their efforts extremely worthy of praise. Otherwise, where would the voiceless and oppressed turn?

I am glad that some of the UNPO members have now joined the UN, especially those nation states that were part of the former USSR. I hope that, although they have now joined the UN, they will continue to support the UNPO and that they will collaborate with various NGO's to reform the UN so that it will have more of the people's participation.

There is another organization called URI—United Religions Initiative—which has collaborated for the past three years so that religious and spiritual leaders can influence the UN to change—not only intellectually and institutionally—but URI hopes for the UN to become spiritual and moral.

I believe the UNPO has a deep moral and spiritual commitment. It has done wonderful work for underrepresented nations and peoples lawfully and nonviolently. I hope in the near future, UNPO will use more arts and cultures as well as religious initiatives, ecumenically and internationally, to awake the public. This would allow the suffering of the voiceless to be overcome. Through the beauty of humanity, we can elevate goodness and truthfulness.

In Buddhism, the Four Noble Truths start with the Truth of suffering, i.e. half of the world population is malnourished, homeless and has been oppressed in various ways—due to the structural violence of social systems and unjust international economic orders which link multinational corporations with arms trades and drug trades as well as the so-called Free Trade—this is not fair at all. The Second Noble Truth in Buddhism is the causes of suffering which are greed, hatred and delusion. In modern terms, greed is represented by capitalism, consumerism, and globalization. Hatred is represented by centralization and non-democratic governments as well as bureaucratic officialdom. Delusion is represented by modern education, which stresses only the head and not the heart. The clever ones are recognized and rewarded while students aren't aware or don't care about social justice and ecological balance.

The Third Buddhist Noble Truth is the cessation of suffering, which is the result of practicing the Fourth Truth, which is the Noble Eightfold Path. In short, the Path is the cultivation of a peaceful mind so that we can reform our consciousness to be less selfish and be critically aware of our self and society. By treading the Path, we become aware of how to restructure society peacefully so that suffering is overcome individually, socially and internationally.

I am grateful that UNPO's efforts are directed to overcoming the suffering of various ethnic minorities and unrecognized nations nonviolently, legally, morally and spiritually. I hope this effort will become more known and will contribute significantly to our world. This is especially relevant this year, the 50th anniversary of the United Nations Universal Declaration of Human Rights. When we turn to the year 2000, I hope UNPO will play an even greater role, especially artistically, culturally, and spiritually—not only for human rights and responsibilities—but to overcome suffering—to restore peace, happiness and beauty—and to strengthen local cultural identities from the homogenization of multinational corporations.

[Sulak Sivaraksa recipient, delivered at the UNPO International Human Rights Conference, Taipei, September 24, 1998.]

TESTIMONY ON
YADANA GAS PIPELINE

My name is Sulak Sivaraksa, of the Middle Temple, barrister-at-law. I would like to testify as president of Kalayanamitra Council which comprises members from around the world whose concern is to make sure that human beings should support each other and advise each other as a voice of conscience. That is what Kalayanamitra really means.

Since April 1997, hundreds of protesting letters have been submitted to Mr. Chavalit Yongchaiyuth, the previous prime minister, by the council's members, some of whom are Nobel laureates on peace, science and literature. Every one of us called for courage and moral stand of the government to ensure peace and happiness of the people in both Siam and Burma, as well as to protect the environment of both countries. We asked them to:

1. Annul the shameful contract with MOGE (Myanmar Oil and Gas Enterprise under former SLORC or SPDC : State Peace and Development Council at present) and its consortium, and legitimize it by inviting Aung San Suu Kyi to become a co-partner as she led the party that won the election.
2. Ask the Burmese Junta to cease all of their human rights abuses.
3. Ask the Burmese Junta to allow freedom in every aspect of life.
4. Ask the Burmese Junta and the Thai government to strictly observe the requirements of the Environmental Impact Assessment (EIA).

Herewith, I would like to hand you three documents:
1. A copy of our letters addressed to Chavalit Yongchaiyuth last

April.

2. A brief report on the history of Kalayanamitra Council and deadly impacts of the gas pipeline project.

3. Our most recent letter to the present Prime Minister that was officially acknowledged.

In June 1997, the issue of the gas pipeline was raised to the People's Tribunal, which was held in Denver. The trial took place almost at the same time with the G8 Summit (as Russia had then just joined).

1. After hearing the case, the court condemned Unocal and Total for their irresponsibility as far as human rights abuses and environmental destruction were concerned. Moreover, by co-partnering with SPDC, they earned a large sum of money, most of which will be used to purchase arms to suppress and kill their own people.

2. The court condemned the American and French governments for their responsibility to allow the two corporations to be based in the countries.

3. The court asked the Thai government to annul the contract they signed with the Burmese regime which is known to be one of the worst administrations in the world because it lacks any legitimacy to rule over the country.

4. The court proposed that a neutral organization be formed to assess the impacts of the construction on the natural balance and the well-being of the people along the pipeline route.

People's Tribunal may lack authority to ask all concerned parties to abide by their rulings, similar to the World Court at the Hague which cannot force defending governments to comply with its rulings. However, even if concerned parties refuse to abide, our judgments are equipped with political legitimacy and morality. A case in hand was a ruling on the US government by the People's Tribunal in which Bertrand Russell was the President who helped to end the Vietnam War.

(I therefore would like to hand over this document of the Tribunal as the second document.)

I would like to ask the government, via this committee, the following question: For what reason have we supported the purchase of gas from Burma, other than that other countries would have taken the opportunity if we had not? Is it true that our country is badly in need of energy for its industries? I would like to ask knowledgeable and concerned authorities to give their opinions on these issues, and if the gas will be used for the benefit of Thai people, or for the benefit of the big multi-national companies and investors. Moreover, according to the contract, it is said that the illegitimate Burmese regime will be able to use the gas as well.

Another relevant fact is our power plant is not to be completed in time for the scheduled commencement of delivery. This means we are now rushing to complete the pipeline and to pay the Burmese regime and its consortium without getting any benefit from the gas. Furthermore, the pipeline will be instrumental for the Burmese regime to crush down strongholds of ethnic groups in their country.

The Thai government has never been concerned about human rights, moral values, and impacts on natural environment, not to mention the legal aspects.

I would like to begin by looking at the problem legally. First of all, SLORC has no legitimacy to govern the country, as they had lost the last general election. Its new name "SPDC (State Peace & Development Council)" signified no change; on the contrary, it signifies a more Orwellian regime.

Members of the National League for Democracy (NLD) won the most seats in the election, but the Junta had detained them and tortured them. They had to flee their country and form their government in exile.

SLORC was somehow comparable to NPKC (National Peace Keeping Council), a junta which seized power from the Thai civilian government in 1991. However, they are worse than the Thai junta as at least the latter allowed civilians to form a government which was composed of people of high calibre and moral concern who could help push through a new and more democratic constitution in a short period of time. One of the Thai coup leaders broke his promise of not taking the prime minister post; he then later accepted it, but was ousted by public uprising even though there were deaths and casualties involved. In stark contrast, every peaceful uprising by the Burmese people has been reacted with brutal violence by the junta, as if law does not exist.

In my opinion, Burma should learn lessons from the former Soviet Union. After the end of World War I, the Soviet Union was praised by all progressive intellectuals as a model of socialist state. George Orwell was the only critic who predicted that the regime would crumble due to its violent measures waged against the people and its lack of moral legitimacy. No one believed in the prediction, although we witnessed it in 1992.

It seems that the Thai government had not been aware of this illegitimacy. For they signed a contract with SLORC, the brutal Junta, and if SLORC were to be demolished, then the contract would go annulled. They may have forgotten that we made a contract during World War II with Petain's government (Petain, Henri Philippe) and previously we had lost a lot of army personnel, weapons and a large sum of money in exchange for the return of Battambong, Seam Reap, Mongkhol Buri, Srisophon and Laos. However, after the war, the new French government refused to recognize the contract we signed with Petain's government, and Siam had to return all the teritories back to France without any gain.

If the NLD and Daw Aung San Suu Kyi can peacefully overturn SLORC's power, she and her party might not recognize the contract we had signed with SLORC. Therefore, the Kalayanamitra Council's request for the Thai government to include the Burmese oppositions in the signing and make it a tri-partite contract is legally commendable.

Moreover, are we aware that we are doing business with a dictatorial regime widely known to be involved with drug trade and which has been using most of the country's resources to purchase arms to suppress their own people, whether they are opposed to them or not? Does the Thai government feel it is right to do so? Are we ready to buy cheap gas reaped from blood and sweat of the Burmese people as well as the ethnic minorities such as Mon, Shan, Karen, Kachin, etc., with no moral consciousness even though the "cheapness" is yet to be substantially proved?

If we are courageous enough to overturn the contract, it is not only that we will be able to save up to one million US$ a day, but the Junta will have lost their biggest revenue and therefore might fall quicker.

Why don't we remember the Buddha's teaching and look at things more interdependently? If we follow his words, we have to try to cultivate the four heavenly abodes inside of us. Namely, we have to cultivate loving kindness (metta), a wish for the happiness and well-being of all beings; compassion (karuna), a wish for all beings to be free from suffering; sympathetic joy (mudita), an empathetic attitude towards those corrupted, and hope that even the brutal SLORC may one day awaken from their ignorance; and equanimity (*upekkha*) which does not literally mean non-engagement but stillness, which is necessary to be cultivated before we can properly treat every being with the three preceding qualities.

I hope that the Thai government will not be blinded by its greed and its desire to buy things cheaply from its neighbors without consideration of how much suffering the action will cause the Burmese, and eventually the people of Kanchanaburi and other provinces whose livelihood will be threatened by the presence of the gas pipeline. The wildlife will suffer from the destruction of the best forest we have. Thai people will feel threatened by the possibilities that the ethnic forces might resort to violence and terrorize the pipeline in Siam. Even though some people are lured by money to believe in the goodness of the project, the majority are well aware of how corrupted and hypocritical the ruling class is.

Siam has been widely accused of looking only for short term benefits from logging in Burma and from exploiting Burmese ethnic groups who fled here; it has been criticized for extorting money from Burmese who wish to live in Siam.

These are serious accusations. Without cooperation from the ruling class, whether it be openly or discreetly, these exploitations would not have occurred. Even if they are not involved with the exploitation, the fact that they disengage themselves from this suffering and allow the exploitation to go on is tantamount to a breach of equanimity.

According to Buddhism, if we always feel a desire to possess every natural power we discover, then that attitude is called greed. If we are confronted with those opposed to the use of power, we should not hate them. We should refrain from thinking and accusing our foes or what they protest because they receive money from foreign agencies, etc.

If we continue to disengage ourselves from acknowledging suffering and not caring how much forest is destroyed, this kind of attitude is ignorance (*avijja*), not equanimity.

Our Prime Minister is an honest person and he often overtly expresses his disgust toward suppressive and dictatorial regimes as he used to suffer from dictators during the 1976 uprising. He even personally declared that he will not visit Burma for the said reason.

I believe that he has properly cultivated equanimity and critical awareness. The fact that he ordered the setting up of this hearing committee on the Yadana gas pipeline proves his wisdom.

The majority of another committee established by the Prime Minister voted that the construction of the gas pipeline could be suspended in the case of *force majoure* and that the Thai government would not be considered breaching the contract and would not be fined. Moreover, the Prime Minister also follows the will of the present constitution and allows the protesters to continue their protest in the forest—a position which is commendable.

All I have said should encourage the committee to opine that this shameful contract be revoked and that this decision would greatly help to uplift the moral legitimacy of the present government and would earn the country praise from international communities. If needed, we might allow the government to set up another committee of lawyers to study seriously whether or not the contract could be revoked with righteous reasons. Otherwise, we would only concern ourselves with the desire for money and economic benefits, and forget that in fact economic prosperity can only be sustained on moral and legitimate operations.

The revocation of the contract can be realized only when the ruling class has enough moral courage and when they have properly cultivated the four heavenly abodes, especially loving kindness and compassion. They would be praised for their sympathy for the sufferers and their wishes to see that every being is free from exploitation and suffering.

By revoking the contract, we would not only revive our prestige, we would also reduce the chance for the brutal government to secure 400 millions US$ every year to purchase arms. When the regime loses their substantial revenue, it would be difficult for them to continue in power and the oppositions with Daw Aung San Suu Kyi would have more chance to win peacefully. The exploitation and human rights abuses in Burma would be reduced or stopped. Even though we could not revive all natural balance in Burma, at least the damage would not increase. This would contribute to a better climate. For Thais, without the gas pipeline, they will feel relieved for the forest is saved, and they would be assured that terrorism against the pipeline would not happen. The abundant forest in Kanchanaburi would also greatly benefit the climate of the whole country.

If a charge is to be raised by the other two multi-national corporations against us, it should be appreciated because the wise would not fear accusations and the results of the trial since they care for justice.

If the government is courageous enough to stand for justice, the majority would stand behind them and all concerned people around the world would bestow on them their support based on two main reasons:

1. The Burmese Junta is brutal and corrupt to the extent that it has been condemned by international communities including the President of the US and Congress from which a resolution was made to prohibit any joint investment with Burmese partners in Burma. Similar resolutions were also issued and adopted by different states and organizations in the US. In addition, the US court has accepted a complaint against Unocal for their investment in the project, which undermines human rights in Burma.

2. The Unocal and Total are multi-national companies whose interest is centered around financial benefits and they are ready to exploit any natural resources found in the name of progress. Blinded by their greed, they have no concern for how people will suffer because of their operation. They buy people, a tactic which has been widely used by their Thai partner, Petroleum Authority of Thailand (PTT) to avoid opposition. Of course, they do not care if forests are to be destroyed and it will hugely affect the survival of wildlife.

With reference to document no.3, you will learn that Unocal's personnel acknowledged that they were well aware of the forced labor in Burma.

As we can now envisage what is right and what is wrong, I hope the Thai government will be courageous enough to pursue justice, the decision of which will eventually bring us honor and pride.

Herewith, I would like to hand you more documents, namely:

1) *Human Rights Yearbook : Burma* by Amnesty International
2) *Total Denial* by Earth Rights International and Southeast Asian Information Network
3) *Burma Beyond the Law* by International Centre Against Censorship
4) *Burma Debate* Vol. IV No. 4 November-December 1997, which

contains testimonies from UN representatives and replies from the Burmese government as well as speeches by Daw Aung San Suu Kyi and UN resolutions on Burma.

5) *Report the Facts*, produced by the Karen government in exile focusing abuses in Tavoy and Thai-Burmese border area.

I hope that these documents will be well read by the committee. I would like now to ask for permission to show a video about human rights abuse in Burma, which was broadcast by Channel 11 to a wide range of public on 11 September 1997.

Thank you for your kind attention. And on the occasion of St. Valentine's day, I look forward to the flourishing of love, compassion and justice.

[The speech was read in Siamese for the committee as established by the Thai Prime Minister to hear information from both the supporters and opposing groups of the Yadana pipeline project at the government house on 14 February 1998.]

BEYOND GEO-ECONOMICS

Reconceptualizing Euro-Asian Relations

I do not wish to thank the Thai government for allowing us to hold our meeting here. It is our right and privilege to do so in any democratic country. As Siam claims to be democratic, its government has no right to interfere with lawful gatherings within the Kingdom. In fact the country is only democratic in form, not in essence. The government recently closed down a lively television program which encouraged free discussion and public participation. Later it closed down many radio networks with similar ideas of free expression. Yet the Prime Minister denied that he was responsible for any of these actions. Likewise he denied that he was interfering with this gathering.

Had he been known as a man who always speaks the truth and stands for democratic principles, plus honesty, I would believe in his words. Indeed, without a great number of foreign participants at this meeting and the formal meeting which is about to take place soon after this, we should not be able to have our deliberations here at all.

However, I would like to thank you for the honor of delivering the keynote address, but I must apologize that my presentation will be somewhat limited. Since I can only speak from a Siamese Buddhist perspective, I am bound somewhat to fail to reflect Asian NGO views. So I ask for your forgiveness.

As you know, March 1-2 will be the first Asia-Europe meeting (ASEM) held in Siam. This so-called summit will hopefully bring together 15 European and 10 Asian governmental leaders. They will discuss economic and political cooperation between the EU and the most important countries in Southeast and East Asia. In this summit the EU is developing a long-term strategy towards the region. This strategy is very much centered around promoting the EU's economic self-interest.

In the past, European-Asian relations were dominated by only one-way traffic: Western domination over the East. Although Siam was not colonized politically, it was colonized economically, educationally and intellectually. This country has not yet developed its independence from the West's economic and intellectual domination.

The age of colonization may be officially over, but recolonization in the name of 'development' is very much in evidence. Many people accept the terms 'underdeveloped,' 'developing' and 'developed' nations without realizing that they were imposed by the former imperial powers. The newer term, 'globalization,' is even more dangerous.

The current issue is no longer the EU versus Asia. It is the rich against the poor: the industrial North against the agricultural South, with some countries like Siam in the middle. The industrial North primarily affects Asia of the South through investment for profit: using manufactured goods as the main item, using the mass media as an effective propaganda tool, selling military equipment and training and bringing toxic waste and pollution in its train. As a result the South loses its natural resources, provides cheap labor and produces agricultural products at prices disadvantageous to small farmers, who pay alarming interest rates for essential credit. In addition, countries in the South lose their indigenous cultures and state sovereignty, increase the internal gaps between rich and poor and suffer from environmental degradation, poverty, hunger, dislocation and the development of urban slums.

The North does not escape. Its people are also addicted to mass culture and consumerism and suffer from pollution and environmental degradation and the loss of fundamental values. Their urban problems include increased crime, homelessness and poverty. Employed people suffer from overwork while the already excessive power of the multinational corporations increases. Individuals lose their sense of meaning in life and their sense of peace.

Let me, in passing, touch on the question of human rights. Although my speech deals mainly with economic, social and cultural rights, which will be ignored by ASEM, I would like to affirm the universal status of the non-derogable rights contained in the International Covenant on Civil and Political Rights, the Convention on torture and similar instruments. These rights are harmonious with the ethical systems of all world cultures, and cannot be undermined by the opportunism of authoritarian governments, almost all of which claim to be democratic.

Speaking now from my Buddhist tradition, I would like to remind all of us that the central teaching of Buddhism is the Four Noble Truths, and that the First Noble Truth is the Truth of Suffering, of the reality and fundamental nature of suffering. If one avoids understanding this then one cannot really practice Buddhism. Global development today appears to celebrate a way of life that not only leads away from understanding the reality of suffering but appears to discourage people from even recognizing its existence. Global development, springing from western civilization, claims to adore life but actually starves it of any real meaning; it endlessly speaks of making people happy but in fact blocks their path to the source of real peace and happiness. It is abundantly clear that the material benefits of modernization and westernization are unfairly distributed to the people of this planet. Industrial capitalism has been built upon the violence of conquest, genocide, slavery, debt and bondage. Extermination continues today, especially that of indigenous and tribal peoples. Exploitation also continues to take new forms, including Third World debt, the economic structures of GATT, NAFTA and the WTO and the structural adjustment policies of the IMF and World Bank. These policies and institutions increase the disparities of income and wealth between the industrialized North and the exploited South. Currently one quarter of the global population living in the North consumes over 60% of the world's food, 85% of the world's wood and 70% of the world's energy. Simultaneously, over one billion people in the South live in absolute poverty, without access to the essentials for survival. Disparities between social classes in both the North and the South are increasing, as are gender disparities; women and children are disproportionately represented among the poorest everywhere in the world.

Inequality and exploitation lead to tension and conflict. Although many conflicts are expressed in ethnic terms, the underlying issues are often class based and rooted in the social structures of the global economic system. As social disparities and resistance increase, people increasingly have to be controlled through violent repression. Thus we have a situation where the global economy becomes more and more a predominantly military economy, with the world's leading nations producing the weapons. The five permanent members of the United Nations Security Council: the US, UK, France, Russia and China, export over 85% of the world's arms. France continues to test nuclear weapons despite world protests.

The proliferation of weapons has created an extremely volatile global situation. More and more regions of the world, from Central America to Africa, to Southern Asia and Eastern Europe are losing even the semblance of law and order. As regions of terror spread across the world 'disappearances,' torture, rape and killing become commonplace. People fear to speak out; they fear for their jobs, their lives, and the lives of their families. These conditions are not unique to the South. There is a dramatic increase in violence in the homes, the streets and the schools of Western industrialized countries. Much of this violence is directed against immigrants, guest workers, people of different races, the poor, children and women.

Resistance and repression cannot be understood at the level of militarism alone. We have to grasp the logic of 'techno-capitalism' and the military-industrial complex. From the beginning technology and capital have been inextricably linked: technological advance determines capitalist competition and growth. Everywhere the process of commoditization and mechanization move simultaneously. There is little research on these issues from a religious perspective.

Techno-capitalism is ultimately illogical, destroying the natural integration of planetary life and threatening its very survival. Subsistence is undermined as people are forced to produce for export markets rather than for their own needs. Tropical forests and coral reefs are destroyed in the name of economic growth and development. Agri-business, industrial manufacturing, nuclear weaponry and toxic dumping pollute the soil, air and water. Around the globe the damming of rivers poses severe threats to and destroys ecosystems and the peoples who have inhabited them, along with their cultures and traditional wisdoms. The twin forces of technology and capitalism are tearing people away from each other by destroying traditional communities. Human relationships are replaced by impersonal commercial, technological and bureaucratic connections. Modernization has increased alienation, distrust and fear among people, making it easier for multinational corporations and international agencies to manipulate and control them.

In the years ahead the corporate control of both human and nonhuman planetary life will broaden and deepen as biotechnology and genetic engineering are more widely used. Already corporations are controlling and altering the genetic materials of plants and animals and claiming patent rights or ownership to these manufactured products. Local producers, including indigenous people and farmers are rapidly losing control of original genetic material. The global biodiversity treaty adopted at the Earth Summit in Rio may, paradoxically, further encourage these trends. We must be wary of 'Green Capitalism': i.e., environmentalism as defined and managed by dominant global interests.

Technology and capital are also making rapid inroads into the sphere of human reproduction. As artificial reproduction advances, human beings, like the earth itself, will lose the capacity to reproduce naturally. There is a close parallel between the conquest of Mother Earth and the conquest of the female body that bears life.

Population control when coupled with modern technology and age-old patriarchal traditions results in sex-selective abortion and female infanticide. In China and India, the two most populous countries in the world, amnio-centesis is routinely used for sex selection, and female fetuses are aborted in large numbers. Many female infants are also killed or abandoned at birth. Already the sex ratios in China and India are skewed in favor of males over females.

There are now movements across the world for peace, social justice and ecology. These include Siamese Buddhist monks ordaining trees to preserve the forest; the struggles of indigenous and tribal peoples against deforestation and the damming of rivers; the struggles of local farmers against biotechnology corporations; protests of relatives, especially wives and mothers, against 'disappearances' etc. These struggles could be better integrated and their common agenda should be firmly placed on a nonviolent and spiritual path. This is the only way they can overcome the violence and destructiveness of the dominant world order.

The teaching we need in order to walk this path already exists. The challenge facing humanity is not the development of more and more technology, markets and bureaucracies, but the spiritual development of wisdom and compassion. From the Buddhist viewpoint all this suffering is directly or indirectly linked with greed, hatred and delusion.

Today, greed is clearly personified in capitalism and consumerism. Human beings are taught to worship money, worldly sciences and technological advance, at the expense of human development and the spiritual dimension of men and women.

Descartes formulated his knowledge of existence in the statement "*cogito ergo sum*"; "I think, therefore I am." I feel that he started the Western dilemma that has now come to the core concept of consumerism, which reformulates that position as: "I buy, therefore I am." Without the power of purchasing, modern people become nobody. And the so-called summit meeting in this country will concentrate mostly on the promotion of economic interest, the encouragement of even more getting and spending.

In Buddhism we could say: "I breathe, therefore I am." We breathe in for the first time as we enter the world from our mothers' wombs and we breathe out for the last time when we expire from life. Yet we do not take care of our daily breathing; we breathe in suffering, anxiety, hatred and greed. One doesn't have to believe in Buddhism. If one is a Christian one can breathe in Christ and be happy. If one is agnostic one can breathe in happiness itself. Through breathing exercises we can be mindful and synchronize our heads and hearts. We will then have understanding and compassion rather than arrogant intellectual knowledge. We can have personal transformation, become less selfish and care more for others. We can also develop critical self-awareness and awareness of social ills, in order to find our true potential for facing suffering both mentally and socially.

From a Buddhist perspective, for human beings to live happily there must be freedom on three levels:

First, is the freedom to live with nature and the environment. We could call this physical freedom. This includes freedom from want and deprivation, and adequate supply of the four basic necessities of life: food, clothing, shelter and medicine. This also includes freedom from natural dangers and the ability to deal with such dangers when they arise.

Second, is freedom in our relationship with fellow humans. We must have social freedom so that we can live safely together without being exploited by others.

But these two kinds of freedom will not be truly effective if they are not connected to the third freedom: inner freedom, or freedom on the personal level. Having physical and social freedom, people must learn how to live independently, to be happy and contented within themselves. The most important kind of development is human development on the personal level leading to inner freedom.

This is a happiness that is independent of externals; with it we are no longer dependent upon exploiting nature or our fellow human beings. We become more and more capable of finding contentment within our own minds and through our own wisdom. The ability to be content without exploiting nature or our fellow humans can also be called the ability to be content independent of natural and social conditions. With a more independent kind of happiness, social and physical freedom will be preserved and strengthened. Human beings will then have the best possible relationship with both the natural environment and human society.

When we talk about inter-faith dialogue, it would have real meaning if people of different faiths and ideologies joined together in working against our common enemies: greed, hatred and delusion.

From a Buddhist standpoint, after the Truth of Suffering, one must go on to the Second of the four Noble Truths, the Truth of the Cause of Suffering, which lies in greed, hatred and delusion. If we can overcome these, either through the Buddhist Noble Eightfold Path or through nonviolent means derived from other traditions, we can easily achieve the Third and Fourth Noble Truths: that of the Cessation of Suffering and of the Way to Achieve the Cessation of Suffering.

With regard to these I am currently working on two new projects to help confront the issues of globalization and to go beyond geoeconomics. The first of these is called Alternatives to Consumerism. The Santi Pracha Dhamma Institute is collaborating with fellow Buddhists, Christians and Muslims in order to identify consumerism as a new demonic religion in global development. We work together, using our various spiritual traditions as well as scientific approaches, to create and identify alternatives to consumerism.

If we do not have an alternative to consumerism our traditional religions will remain at the periphery of the new dominant value system that reduces human beings to the mercy of greed. In today's world the desire to earn more and more money and consume more and more unnecessary goods is a dominant force at the expense of spiritual growth and contentment. Through the clever use of advertisements and media the multinational corporations strongly influence, and in may cases mercilessly exploit, people around the world. Nightly news programs and so-called entertainment project violence into our homes. Television advertisements lull us away from this violence and delude us, using greed and lust as a means to stir our thirst to possess more and more.

Our second project, the Spirit in Education Movement (SEM), responds to the problem that in this dissolute modern world there is little time and thought for education of the heart as well as the mind. Mainstream Western education concentrates on the intellect and is becoming increasingly businesslike and competitive. As Eastern countries jump gaily on the consumer bandwagon their educational-systems emulate the narrow unconnected fields of Western education. Unbalanced modern education regularly produces shortsighted and self-centered "new" ideas, often borrowed out of context from old traditions and indigenous wisdoms. Hence the challenge for alternative education.

With help from concerned friends SEM was formed to respond to these challenges. We aspire to offer a spiritually based, ecologically sound, holistic alternative to mainstream education with its narrow, unconnected fields. We also aspire to benefit people, initially mainly Asians, by increasing individual and collective confidence in our traditional heritage. We will aid individuals and groups who re-sist structural violence and greed to build up courage, confidence and compassion, and give long-term support for their projects.

For me, SEM is one of the very positive responses to the next phase of global development. Unfortunately, those attending the so-called Summit on March 1-2 will not understand either this philosophy or my commitment to it. I hope, however, that those of you who want to reconceptualize beyond Cartesian intellectual compartmentalization will be sympathetic to our project. I hope that some of you who are concerned with education for the spiritual dimension of global order beyond geoeconomics would be willing to offer comments, criticisms and suggestions. Indeed, if some of you were willing to participate in our programs, I would be very happy indeed.

I will no longer elaborate on these two projects. If any of you are interested in either of them, you may read about them in my new book just published today to honor you all. Its title is **Modern Thai Monarchy and Cultural Politics.** It also deals with human rights from the Buddhist perspective.

In conclusion, I hope and expect that this NGO Forum will act as the voice of the people in face of the threats to culture and economic integrity which the agenda of globalization repre-sents. I would encourage you to dig deep in your own traditions for forms of cultural resistance to the destructive march of consumerism and techno-capitalism.

[Sulak Sivaraksa gave this keynote speech at the February 27-29 NGO Conference preceding the March 1-2 Asia-European Union Summit 1996, in Bangkok.]

A CHALLENGE TO
THE 2ⁿᵈ ASEM MEETING

The world community today is facing a great crisis that demands a revolution no smaller than the one that led Europe out of the middle ages to the modern era. As you all may be aware, crisis also means opportunity. So, as leaders in this time of history, you are all responsible for making the right decision to turn our crisis into a new opportunity for redirecting human society from common disaster into common good and well-being—not only for human beings, but also for all other beings on earth. The time for positioning the human being as the center from which to dominate the rest of nature has gone.

A common mistake of both European and Asian leaders has been their making economic growth the supreme aim of their respective countries.

Western Europe has humanized its approach to some extent by some measures of income distribution, democratic institutions, and human rights standards as well as constant improvement in environmental regulations. But this is not enough, as it still functions within the growth-oriented framework and encourages excessive consumerism—not to mention its arms production and sales of arms worldwide. Moreover, fellow human beings and natural resources are being exploited in other parts of the world. This trend needs to be reversed, along with the reduction of the West's material standard of living which consumes more than its fair share of the world's natural resources. New moral frameworks need to be formulated both at the structural and personal level. For example, if one considers the effects of owning a private car, it would be morally wrong if all Chinese and Indians owned one.

The irony is that SEA and other Asian countries have been crudely following this outdated model of unlimited growth-oriented development without much care for human rights and environmental regulations. Hence the human rights abuse and environmental destruction all over the region amidst the once high times of economic growth. Accompanying the growth is women trafficking, child labor, discrimination against ethnic minorities, etc. A most recent shameful case is the Yadana Gas Pipeline that has cut a gash up to 10 kilometers wide across Burma, relocating around 13 ethnic villages and largely built with "porterage" or forced labour. The project will also be the largest source of income generation for the military government of Burma. Largely financed by French giant Total and American Unocol, this kind of action would cause an outcry in their own countries. As the pipeline reaches the Thai border, local people in Kanchanaburi are strongly protesting the pipeline in the hope of saving some of the last remaining forests in Siam. But when the action get hot the army is sent in, and the arrests begin.

From a spiritual perspective this kind of development does not truly benefit any one, even when the rich get richer their quality of life gets poorer. In the rich sectors of society there is increasing unemployment, disregard for older people and disintegration of community and family. Individuals become lonely and selfish, without meaning in life. Even though some of the poor may get a little trickle down of material benefit, others are starving as the victims of large modern development projects. Moreover, the traditional sustainable ways of life are destroyed and the people become discontented.

As leaders, maybe you are becoming aware that the transnational corporations (TNC) are the new monsters that need to be tamed and kept under control; otherwise the governments will just be puppets to serve its vested interests. With bases in many countries its power transcends nations and it strategically plans activities in areas with low labor costs and favorable conditions. The TNC is uncaring of the social and cultural damage left behind, and it moves when it suits them to more profitable locations. Environmental concern diminishes in remote areas with inadequate legislation. TNC, in cahoots with the media, is creating a never-ending demand for consumer goods. The TNC view of development, supported by both ASEAN and the EU, is an eternal search for new markets to exploit with little regard to negative consequences. It is the moral choice of the governments whether one is on the side of the people to whom you are accountable or to the servants of the TNC. Throughout the world today the environment is fighting back. There is strong evidence that eco-systems around the world are breaking as we see phenomena like falling water tables, flooding, and climate change. In short the development model promoted by the west is not only unsustainable, it is devastating our planet. We can no longer stand this western throw-away lifestyle. The global economy is outgrowing the earth's eco-systems.

From a Buddhist viewpoint, and I am sure other spiritual perspectives would agree, a more frugal lifestyle that is close to a natural environment is not only necessary for the survival of the earth but is more beneficial as happiness comes from reduction of greed, hatred and delusion, and not from satisfying these desires. Simple living gives us more chance for inner development which is a must for a good quality of life.

I would like to emphasize again that we are all part of a new revolution, and it is our common responsibility to redirect our collective *karma* by moving from a common disaster brought about by exploiting each other and destroying our planet. The new direction is the path of spiritual enlightenment, compassion for each other, and care for Mother Earth.

[This speech was delivered by Sulak Sivaraksa at the opening ceremony at the Royal Commonwealth Society, London on 31st March, 1998 for Asia Europe: People's Forum, prior to the 2nd ASEM meeting.]

THE RIGHT TO SELF-DETERMINATION

A Buddhist Approach

As expressed in Article I of the United Nations Charter, and developed in General Assembly resolution 1514, the principle of equal rights and self-determination of peoples is fundamental to the UN human rights agenda. But recently, there have been a number of governments, particularly in Asia, questioning the concept of universal Human Rights in the light of cultural variations. Rather than dealing with the right of self-determination, I will seek to counter such statements by using the Buddhist approach to human rights. Indeed the right to self-determination is, first of all, the right of a people to choose its form of government or the nature of the state. Article 5 of the Universal Declaration of the Right of Peoples adopted in Algiers in 1956, states that: "Every people has an unquestionable and inalienable right to self-determination to determine its political status freely and without interference." This principle applies to the peoples of Western Sahara, East Timor and Tibet, to the indigenous peoples of the world and indeed many others.

The Vienna Declaration and Program of Action of the World Conference on Human Rights in 1993, which was adopted by consensus, reaffirmed the universality and inseparability of human rights:

All Human Rights are universal, indivisible, interdependent and interrelated. The international community must treat Human Rights globally in a fair and equal manner on the same footing and with the same emphasis. While the significance of national and regional particularities and various historical,

cultural and religious backgrounds must be borne in mind,
it is the duty of states, regardless of their political, economic
and cultural systems, to promote and protect all human rights
and fundamental freedoms.

In other words, if there is a conflict between universal human
rights and regional particularities, the former must prevail over the
latter. The Bangkok Non-governmental Declaration of Human Rights
of 1993 also stated that:

We affirm the basis of universality of human rights which
accord protection to all humanity. While advocating cultural
pluralism, those cultural practices which derogate from
universally accepted human rights, including woman's rights,
must not be tolerated.

The notion of human rights usually has four characteristics.
First, it is a legal, legitimate claim of individual persons and people.
Second, these rights are politically powerful as grounds of grievances.
Third, they are often grounds to protest against the "powers that
be" to reform policies and redress social justice. Thus, fourth, the
entire atmosphere in which human rights questions occur is
adversarial—people against government. Here in this atmosphere
of rupture between the ruler and the ruled, people, often individual
persons, initiate the legal and political protest against the government.
Human rights are at the centre of the fight for justice and the
right to self-determination of the indigenous peoples *vis-a-vis* the
powers that be. These people have the legitimate right for self-
determination whether they live in the slums of a cosmopolitan
city, a vast country like Tibet, East Timor or Western Sahara.
People like Lee Kuan Yew of Singapore or Suharto of
Indonesia, who claim that the concept of human rights is not within
Asian culture, are not only hypocritical, but also have no awareness
of the scope and subtlety of Asian tradition. The hypocrisy of these
leaders whose actions brutally abuse the dignity of ordinary people
shows a failure to understand their own roots. The result is only
clinging to the form or ceremony of being Asian. Whilst free societies
depend on trust between the people, dictatorships try to destroy
any trust between citizens.
Lee Kuan Yew is supposed to adhere to the Chinese concept

while Suharto claims to be a practising Muslim. For a Muslim, there is no need to examine currently prevailing *sharia* definitions of human and citizen rights. In other words, what is known as the Universal Declaration of Human Rights is by no means alien to Islam but is grounded in the Quaranic notion of a common human theology (*fitrah*), couched in an Islamic idiom of moral universalism which predates much of the Western discourse on human rights.

The Chinese claim that in their world view there is no regard for the individual persons, only communal sociality or the solidarity by virtue of a homocosmic continuum. There is no legitimation of people's protest with their assertion of human rights, only the ruler's (or ruling party's) duties to treasure and care for the popular welfare by virtue of the sympathetic exigency of human nature. A government more for the people than of them was Mencius's vision which summed up the tradition concerning the matter. Such a populist government consists of at least three characteristics, the people were: a) the most precious, b) the royal object of the most concern, and c) the heavenly test to confer the mandate to rule.

It is a sad comment on the world today that the universal consensus on human rights (synonymous with the supreme value of common folks) is universally neglected. Just ask which nations are implementing Mencius's plan or adhere to the Universal Declaration of Human Rights. Mr. Clinton praises the Tibetan rights for self-determination and laments the persecution by the Chinese. Clearly, however, trade with China is much more important to him than the Tibetan rights. Western business people will jump into Burma now that Aung San Suu Kyi has been released. But the human rights situation in Burma is still very bad and Suu Kyi herself may be in great personal danger. This worldwide political hypocrisy—paying lip-service to human rights—manifests itself in worldwide brutalities towards common folk, as repeatedly documented by Amnesty International. Mencius' scathing words of warning apply to all of us, especially the worldwide political hypocrisy.

Thousands of years of dictatorial brutality in Asia have formed personal habits that are hard to change, as is dramatically demonstrated in China, Tibet, Burma, Indonesia and East Timor—just to mention a few. While self-determination in that region has been denied by dictatorial regimes, governments do nothing to stop the trafficking of women and girls into brothels in other countries. At least SLORC in Burma and the PRC government do not try to hide their practices. In the case of the PRC, they hid their practice in Tibet but not in the recent Tianamen massacre. It is encouraging that the PRC are now publicly announcing regrets over the Tianamen incidents. The PRC claims to learn from the Confucian teaching. If they learned from Mencius, they and other world leaders would be less hypocritical.

Speaking as a Buddhist, the principal contribution of Buddhism to the question of rights and ethics is the stress it places on the psychological dimensions of human action. For instance, according to Ven. P.A. Payutto, a leading Siamese commentator on Buddhism and social isssues, well-developed human beings are free of the five kinds of *macchariya* (covetousness or possessiveness):

1. *Macchariya* of locality and country;
2. *Macchariya* of family or group, including ethnic and religious group;
3. *Macchariya* of material wealth;
4. *Macchariya* of social class or caste, including race, skin, colour, etc;
5. *Macchariya* of knowledge or learning, including intellectual achievements.

The right to self-determination as it applies specifically to Tibet, East Timor and Western Sahara is very much linked to the five possessiveness (*macchariya*), mentioned above. If people, especially the aggressors, could develop their attitude to be free of covetousness or possessiveness, they would understand that self-determination of indigenous peoples are as basic as any other human rights.

True human development, according to the Ven. Payutto, leads to the complete eradication of these five kinds of possessiveness. He argues that the time has come to do away with all possessiveness in order to save the world from the threat of war and destruction. In the present time, however, he sees the opposite happening. Unlike technological development, which has provided for increased interdependence and communication, humans at the present time have become more aggressively competitive, looking for personal survival and personal prosperity at the expense of others. Within this context, human rights do serve to hold the world together to some degree within its divisiveness.

From a Buddhist perspective, the establishment of freedom and happiness for human beings must have three levels. The first freedom is the freedom to live with nature and the environment. We could call this physical freedom. This is freedom from want and deprivation: an adequate supply of the four basic necessities of life: food, clothing, shelter and medicine. This also includes freedom from natural dangers and the ability to deal with such dangers when they arise.

The second freedom exists in our relationship with fellow humans. We must have social freedom so that we can live safely together without being exploited by others, including not being exploited by any government or state. From a Buddhist perspective, a government or state is only a form recognized by the people for their own benefit. If the state loses its legitimacy by not promoting and protecting human rights and self-determination, it too will not last forever. This can be seen clearly in the cases of the former Soviet Union recently, and British India earlier on. Indeed, the nation state in its most common form was born in 18th and 19th century Europe and the United States, along with the concept of the individual. The basic idea is that the state is composed of, and represents, the people or nation.

The subsequent export of the idea and institution of the nation state by colonialism constitutes probably the major imposition of western values on the rest of the world. Incidentally, those governments which attack the notion of human rights and the individual as a western invention are remarkably subdued in their criticism of the idea of the state. Indeed, unless self-determination by common force is taken seriously, the state itself will lose its capacity for self-determination too, as the international corporation will become more and more powerful in relation to the state. And they will direct the state for the benefit of their corporation so that they are diverted to worship the new religion of consumerism, which is dominated by greed.

From a Buddhist point of view, to fight against a dictator state is in fact difficult. To fight against power and anger is difficult enough. But to fight against consumerism and international corporations is even more difficult, because it is fighting against greed. To use social engineering, politics and laws against this is not enough. One will need spiritual depth and human development at its best for the protection and implementation of human rights and self-determination. But these two kinds of freedom will not be truly effective if they are not connected to inner freedom. This is freedom on the personal level. Having physical and social freedom, people must learn how to live independently, to be happy and contented within themselves. The most important kind of development is human development on the personal level leading to inner freedom. This is a happiness that is independent of externals; with it we are no longer dependent on exploiting nature or our fellow beings. We become more and more capable of finding contentment within our hearts and through our own wisdom. The ability to be content, without exploiting nature or our fellow humans can also be called the ability to be content, independent of natural and social conditions. With a more independent kind of happiness, social and physical freedom will be preserved and strengthened. Human beings will then have the best possible relationship with both the natural environment and human society.

If Buddhists are to make a meaningful contribution to world peace and liberation of the modern world from violence and oppression, they must confront the three root causes of evil: greed, hatred and delusion, not only in the individual person, but also in their social and structural dimensions. All practising Buddhists must develop the right-mindfulness that allows them to deal with these issues at the deepest levels.

His Holiness the Dalai Lama has provided an inspiring model for many of us to continue to oppose evil and oppression while cultivating internal seeds of peace and maintaining love for our enemies. I am convinced that one day Tibet will be free from Chinese domination and destruction. At that time, perhaps, it will offer us an example of Buddhist democracy or Dharmic socialism. Similarly, I am convinced that the moral courage of Aung San Suu Kyi will one day free the people of Burma from the SLORC military junta.

With *kalayanamitta* (good friends) in the International Network of Engaged Buddhists, which is linked to the Buddhist Peace Fellowship and other similar organisations in the US, Europe and Japan, I have been privileged to work for peace and challenge structures of oppression in Siamese society and other parts of the world. Despite social and political oppression and the destruction of the environment, much of my vision for renewing society and for human liberation is partially sustained by the support and community of working with *kalayanamitta*.

According to Buddha, *kalayanamitta* are the most important external elements for everyone. We need to have good friends and companions to learn from, to help develop ourselves and society towards peace and justice, starting with peace and justice within. Once we can restructure our consciousness to be less selfish, then, with *kalayanamitta*, we can surely reconstitute our societies to be free from oppression and exploitation. This may not be easy, but it is possible. This development goes beyond the Human Rights Conventions and points to a positive direction beyond the simple, or not so simple, eradication of unskillful actions. This eradication is meant to provide the groundwork for the development of a fuller spiritual life, a reintegration, in Taoist terms, into the higher levels lost before the discussion of justice was ever necessary.

[from the Question of Self-Determination published by UNPO, the Hague, 1996.]

HONG KONG

Transfer of Powers

Great Britain's return of Hong Kong to China on July 1, 1997 is right and proper. We must realize that Hong Kong has always been a part of China. Now China will determine Hong Kong's future. I sincerely hope that China treats the people of Hong Kong with gentleness and skillfulness, that the people of Hong Kong are allowed freedom of expression and the freedom of democratic participation. Hong Kong has the opportunity to be a good model for the way China treats Tibet.

If China's approach to Hong Kong is dictatorial and without respect for basic human rights, the people of Hong Kong will suffer, the people of mainland China will suffer, and the people of Tibet will suffer. If China follows its present course of development, giving only lip service to socialism, Hong Kong will become a gateway for materialism to enter the mainland. There will be greater and greater gaps between rich and poor and further destruction of China's environment. I therefore hope that China responds to the growing threat of multinational corporations with skill and very great care.

I feel that China can learn some significant lessons from the people of Tibet. The Tibetan people have a rich and deep spiritual tradition that seems to be lacking in present day China, as well as Hong Kong. I recently met with His Holiness the Dalai Lama on his visit to meet President Clinton. His Holiness has made it clear that he does not seek independence for Tibet, only autonomy.

China's treatment of Tibet is one example of how it deals with people within its borders. China's treatment of Hong Kong will be another example. If China's future treatment of Hong

Kong and Tibet is skillful, fair and just, I am sure that Taiwan will be prepared to rejoin the motherland.

In this sense, China must be prepared to treat the nations around her borders, nations such as Siam, Burma and Vietnam, as partners. China must not have an imperial attitude. China is not the Big Brother of Asia. China must treat its neighbors fairly and not, for example, bully smaller countries who open their doors to His Holiness the Dalai Lama. But if China is prepared to be a partner and a friend to the other nations of Asia, then all Asians will be able to work together in building regional networks to resist the influences of the multinational corporations that preach consumerism at the expense of the world's poor. Then a genuine end will be put to the colonial period.

In respect to your question of whether colonialism left anything positive for the people of Asia, the legal system left by the British is not perfect but, at least, is based upon principles of rule of law. The modern education system is seriously flawed. It lacks a spiritual dimension and therefore encourages a society that neglects the poor, that places greater emphasis on material develoment at the expense of moral development. At this point, I cannot say if China will be able to improve Hong Kong's system of education.

Although Siam was never colonized politically, it lost its extra-territorial rights to the West which meant that it could only have a 3% import duty. Western citizens were not subject to Thai courts. Siam struggled through many decades before realizing economic and judicial independence. Yet, recently, Siam, by following the examples of the West, has subjected itself to intellectual and cultural colonization. I am afraid that Siam is now under a shadow imperialism imposed by multinational corporations, the World Bank, the IMF, and the World Trade Organization. And Siam is, unfortunately, not the only country in this predicament. Even though many countries in Asia gained independence more than a half century ago, they still face the threat of colonialization. Hong Kong, while not gaining independence, will at least not be a colony of a European power.

Consumerism promotes a monoculture and so is a dictatorial communism. Only with democratic processes, with the full participation of all people, with respect given to indigenous cultures and the rights of indigenous people, and with harmony toward the natural environment, can we all go into the 21st century meaningfully and positively. I must add that this cannot be mere rhetoric or wishful thinking. We must work hard for alterna-tive economics, alternative politics, and alternative education. These are the principles that I humbly occupy myself with, and that we must all occupy ourselves with, as Hong Kong is returned to China, and as we see an end to the era of colonialization.

GENEROSITY OF THE SELF

The Journey of Cultivating Compassion

This interview was conducted immediately following a weekend intensive course at the Naropa Institute, where students explored the obstacles to awakening of the heart within a context of social action. Sulak spoke about the importance of generosity of the self, giving whatever one might have in the form of time, money, commitment, compassion... the purpose of which goes beyond any social action into the journey of cultivating one's own compassion.

Sulak has been one of Southeast Asia's foremost spiritually-based social activists for many years, speaking out for human rights and environmental issues, and the protection of indigenous peoples and wildlife. Most recently, he has been demonstrating to stop the Burmese Yadana pipeline from entering Thailand and destroying the rainforests, and disbanding the elephants who live in their natural environment. Sulak faced a court trial May 13 for peacefully protesting, and the results are still uncertain as of press date.

Thank you, Sulak for your time and this interview. While we know it is not so easy to be this brief, could you please give our readers an introduction to who you are and what you are doing?

My name is Sulak Sivaraksa and I am from Bangkok. I run an organization called Spirit in Education Movement. I am also involved with the International Network of Engaged Buddhists, where we are trying to bring Buddhists to be aware that in our tradition, it is not enough only to sit in meditation, but we should also be concerned with social issues. The Spirit in Education Movement means that mainstream education has only developed an intellectual power; education must also be developed in our hearts. People should be aware of the suffering in the world, and use compassion to overcome suffering nonviolently.

Many who are Christian, Muslim, Hindu, Jews and other religious traditions are looking for alternatives to consumerism. We need to look into our cultural roots in our own traditions. In my country, we support traditional medicines, traditional arts and crafts. This is the gist of what I am doing. I am a family man with three children... it is all described here in this book—you should get a copy! **Loyalty Demands Dissent.**

The Association for Traditional Studies (ATS) is focused on preserving, documenting and ensuring the survival of the art and knowledge of traditional peoples. We believe their skills hold many of the solutions to the issues our planet faces today and will continue to face in the next century. What kind of role does working to preserve traditional arts and knowledge play in the work that you do?

This question is very near to my heart because there is so much monoculture in the contemporary world. Furthermore, a kind of fundamentalism pervades: "Only my religion; only my tradition." I don't feel this is helpful! In the present age, people tend to think that problems are solved through social engineering, that the quality of life is improved by the advancement of technology.

If we are to move to the next century positively, we need to understand our traditional arts, crafts, and special traditions; we need to reconnect to our roots, our land, and understand our ancestors. All these appear in the folklore of various traditions, spiritual as well as medical. So, firstly, by preserving our link with tradition, it will help to make people aware of the so-called modern, scientific technological solutions, which may be either useful, or harmful. Remember that, the harmful effect is much worse than people realize. Even though traditional arts, crafts, religions, and spirituality have been looked down upon since the age of enlightenment, it is encouraging that people are aware that something deep, and wonderful is being preserved. So, firstly, awaken the populace to understand the shortcomings of this tendency toward mindless social engineering. And secondly, be aware of any tradition which is still alive and support it in a meaningful way, resurrecting any which we see are declining. This is what I do in my country.

I also started an ashram that is just 30 km outside of Bangkok. Bangkok is now supposed to be really modern. It is a concrete jungle full of pollution, traffic jams, and slums. But the ashram that we started from scratch thirteen years ago grows trees and herbal plants, and we cultivate nonchemical vegetables. We use traditional medicines, meditation practice, and support yoga and Taichi practice. This is just one example of how people in Bangkok and the international community can come to enjoy a genuine revival in spirituality, in the natural environment, and learn how certain arts and crafts can be carried out beautifully, mindfully, naturally, compassionately, and harmoniously.

We support various other practices from the ashram. For example, Buddhist monks are now more involved in cultivating traditional rice-growing (no chemical), and they are now reviving traditional medicine. The Indian experts on Aryuraveda have come to us and found that Indian theory is more developed; but our lineage of practice has not been broken. The monks have been, and still are, the custodians of our traditional medicine. This not only includes herbs, but also psychotherapy treatment. What you can learn from the various ethnic groups is tremendous folk wisdom, and craftsmanship, which so far has been looked down upon by the mainstream.

So, my job is to support this, and to try to learn from the tribal peoples. At the same time, I try to talk to the mainstream so that they can at least understand and respect, so that hopefully it would be something they could be proud of.

To accomplish this, I use the Buddhist concept of interconnectedness. We invite people to come each year to participate in an international conference, so that they can evaluate our arts and crafts. With their voices, **our** people will listen. So you need these different kinds of voices, interconnected in these ways, north and south. In these small ways, this is how I work in Siam.

What traditional ways are being lost in Siam today with the indigenous peoples and the Thais?

Indigenous peoples have been looked down upon, first of all, by the Thai mainstream. That is why I do not use the word 'Thailand' because in my country, we are not just Thai (although Thais are about 90% of the population). We are comprised of Muslims, Malay (4-5%), and various ethnics that call themselves

Mao, Mong, Karen... from whom we can learn. We have this idea of them being backward, just hill tribes. This kind of attitudes is destructive.

Then we tried to make them Thai. We even made them Buddhists (but not in a very attractive way) so that they would give up their spirit worship. But to me, that has been a very important element of their culture for hundreds of years. They had to give up their traditional dress, they lost their community, and they have now become involved with money instead of barter. We introduced foreign medicine.

All of this, on the whole, I see as very harmful. Not only did the Thai government introduce Buddhist culture, but the missionaries came and made them Christian. They told them, "Look down upon your own culture! Only one God! There are no other gods," and so on. This for me, on the periphery, is very drastic among the minorities.

Over the last 150 years, although we were not colonized politically, we were colonized intellectually and economically. And we were made to feel inferior to the west and so we tried to catch up with the west. We became intellectualized and compartmentalized. We began to follow blindly western medicine and education. Western education and medicine look upon the human being as a kind of machine, merely a physical being, nothing spiritual. The result is that we become alienated from our own culture. Although we do pay lip service to Buddhism, we also pay lip service to our culture. But we are uprooted from our cultures. That is why I feel we must come back to the essence of Buddhism and at the same time, bring the forms that are appropriate for the modern world. The forms that are appropriate to the modern world must have roots in our traditions, in our culture, and not be alienated from those roots.

How do you see this transition happening so as not to go back to the old, but bringing something from the past into the present?

It is important to understand the past without blindly romanticizing it. Through critical analysis, we'll find both positive and negative elements. Even if some of the positive aspects may not seem appropriate for the modern world, we can still try, without being judgmental, to apply it meaningfully and with humility. The wisdom which comes from traditional cultures helps us to be humble and interrelated with nature and other humans.

Our readers are always interested in hearing about traditional arts and skills. Can you share with us a few examples of skills that people of the traditional spiritual path have and the 'modern world' doesn't have or might want to develop that you have come across over the years?
I feel that the traditional people I have met everywhere have a very simple lifestyle. Modern people have a very complicated lifestyle. A very wasteful lifestyle! Our lifestyle is harmful to our self, to our family, to the environment and to the majority of people in the world. There is a book called **How The Other Half Dies**. The other half dies because of the modern lifestyle. In the northern hemisphere, the middle class consumes wastefully, consumes in such a harmful way. Even the television we look at is full of violence, full of advertisement promoting greed, hatred, delusion, lust and so on. I feel that even in the family, the more we have television sets, the more we do not talk to each other! The more we are attached to television and computers, we lose that being together.

Whereas, the indigenous people, the tribal people, those who are supposed to be poor and 'backward', they relate meaningfully in the family. They exhibit an equality amongst one another as well as respect; they love and care for their ancestors. Modern people tend to look down upon the aged, the sick, and the poor, by putting the sick somewhere and the aged somewhere else.

I think the holistic approach creates a simpler lifestyle. They care for seven generations, which is also common to the native Americans in this culture. We care for our ancestors who help us, pray for us, cultivate us, and care about the children to come. I think there is a tremendous amount that we can learn from them!

Whether it be the monks of Christianity, Buddhism, or Daoism, the elders of tribes, or the shamans of indigenous people, all were viewed as repositories of knowledge. They were the people with skills and understanding of the arts of their peoples. What do you see as the connection between spiritualism and the traditional arts and knowledge of cultures?
This is what I meant about a 'holistic' approach. Within spiritual traditions, one is not compartmentalized, but is viewed as a totality. Traditional medicine is preventative as well as curative. Cure comes not only at the physical level, but at the mental and

spiritual level as well. Charms, dolls, prayers, and holy water are all used to promote health. The medicine man, monk, and shaman care for every one as an individual. You don't prescribe for the whole world!

At the same time, one must realize that sometimes, the tradition gets stuck in forms. For instance, in the Tibetan tradition, if you want to learn medicine, you have to also learn meditation—which is good. But at the same time, this concentrated meditation takes some seven years, seven months and seven days. Most people cannot take that kind of time. Although it should be ideal, if somebody wants to take seven 'months or weeks, they should be able to learn something from that traditional art—in a holistic way, for the benefit of others.

Many young people are turning away from the traditional because the system is too slow for them or the language too awkward. Some of us are trying to link the two. The elderly also need to learn to respect the young. In some of the old traditions, like Confucianism, there is a tendency to be a little patriarchal, where women have been given an unequal role; on the other hand, in some tribes, Buddhism has been positive for women. Even so, Buddhism developed as exploitative to women and this must be changed. But not changed to suit the Women's Liberation Movement here! Rather changed back to the roots, under the Bodhi tree, where men and women can sit as equals. This is what I call radical conservatism. We must conserve but at the same time, we must be radical with certain aspects of the tradition.

Do you feel that a cultures' knowledge and skills help define its spiritualism, or that spiritualism helps define its knowledge and skills? The obvious answer is both, but what is the balance of these two?
I feel that you need a balance. In some traditions, later development separated the spiritual from the traditional arts and skills. Although today's arts, crafts, and paintings may still be traditional, they often have become too concerned about money. When art is created just for monetary gain, it has lost its spirit.

Spirituality means that the artist, the craftsman, and the object created are interconnected. I see that loss in many of the traditional crafts. I think we can challenge the demonic religion of consumerism, the godless development of mega-technology, the computer age...

How important is preserving the natural environment of people in order to protect their culture?

These go hand in hand. Without the natural environment, people are alienated from nature. Once they are alienated from nature, the craft they produce may be traditional in form, but it has lost its spirit, its naturalness. To be natural is to be normal; to be normal is also spiritual. You cannot just cut down all the trees... and you cannot just have a few trees for show. You must have real forests, real parks, everything real. The animals, the elephants, all this... must be real. They must grow naturally. All these animals must be natural—so must we. That is why, when we are uprooted from our traditional spiritual background, we become unreal, a mechanical being. This results in alienation. And once we are alienated from our tradition, from our culture, from our roots, we even become alienated from our family and friends.

The web of interdependence between the environment, spiritualism, and traditional skills is tightly interwoven. Do you see areas of ATS, with its focus on preservation of knowledge, and your work, with its focus on spiritualism, working together to make a bigger impact?

I think the best thing that we can learn from each other is that neither is the answer. In this day and age, we must see the inter-connection. We need to have on going dialogue and mutual respect. With respect and dialogue, we can become friends. True friendship means that we can be critical of each other, while at the same time help each other. With this as our aim, I am quite sure that in the future we may have something in common.

[from **Traditional Studies Journal** Vol. 3 Issue 2, Boulder, Colorado, USA 1998.]

SULAK EXPLAINS HIS WORK
TO KOREAN NGOs

I'm very grateful that many of you have come, despite very fine weather outside. Since I'm addressing Buddhist groups, I ought to tell you about the International Network of Engaged Buddhists. In general, one can divide Buddhists into two groups, not Mahayana and Hinayana, but those who claim to be Buddhists for a long time in Asia and those who have now become Buddhists for the first generation, mostly in Europe and America. I believe that both have particular, yet different, problems.

Many of newly converted Buddhists in Europe and North America want to be peaceful and enjoy their mediation practice. Since most of these new Buddhists came from white middle and upper classes, there is often little concern about social injustice in their own country. The prevailing attitude is, "I'm O.K. Let me take care of my own practice." They don't realize that their own classes are in fact oppressing the suffering majority in their own country and in the world.

For the last twenty years, I've been visiting the West and challenging these new Buddhists to see that what they practice is only one aspect of Buddhism which could be indeed considered selfish. Yet Buddhism teaches us to be selfless and to confront suffering. This is the first of the Four Noble Truths.

However, there are changes developing in America. The Buddhist Peace Fellowship which has been established for 20 years and have chapters in most big cities in the US. Their purpose is to be engaged in confronting the suffering in society. The Berkeley Zen Center is now devoting one day a month for black and Mexican Buddhists who don't want to join the white Buddhists in their meditation practices. Three years ago the Buddhist Peace Fellowship established "BASE" (Buddhist Alliance for Social Engagement).

For the past three years I have been teaching at a Buddhist university in Boulder, Colorado called Naropa Institute. I have been telling the faculty that unless they teach their students in the traditional Buddhist way (and not in the western way)—whatever they call Buddhism will not be Buddhism. They engage with those who have HIV and other social ills.

However, Naropa's program of teaching is very spiritual. They always include meditation with teaching. After I encouraged them to start a course on socially engaged Buddhism, they set up an M.A. degree course under that title. In order to get this degree, students are expected to confront and overcome suffering in the Buddhist way.

Lastly, Sharpham College was established in England two years ago. Twelve students come each year to engage in study, (philosophy, psychology, music, art and yoga), voluntary work in the local town, and community living. Although meditation is a main part of the program, they also need to understand contemporary issues and how to use mindfulness in order to confront suffering. Nearby Schumacher College has been operating for about 10 years. Schumacher was the first British who wrote on Buddhist economics. Last year I taught a course on Buddhist economics, but there are 2-4 week courses offered in the areas of ecology, science and spirituality.

I have presented a picture to show how Buddhism in the North (or West) is evolving. Buddhists have now become involved or engaged in society from the Buddhist perspective. The North, of course, includes Japan. I have been going to Japan for twenty years. Each time I talk to Japanese Buddhists I tell them how beautiful and great is their tradition; unfortunately it is declining gracefully because they only look after their temples and funeral services, and make a lot of money from them.

But, I ask them don't you care that Japanese successful economic development is the result of destruction of the environment and exporting pollution to South East Asia? Don't you care that you import cheap labor from other parts of Asia, including prostitution?

However, during the last ten years more groups of Japanese Buddhists have now changed, and together with us have founded the International Network of Engaged Buddhists. The Buddhist in the modern world cannot remain in his own national or rural community. She must understand the structural violence in society and the unjust international economic order. Traditional Buddhists in South East Asia are also included in this social engagement. Theravada monks usually teach people to practise the Five Precepts: not to kill, not to steal, not to have sexual misconduct, not to tell lie, not to have intoxicants. Teaching people to be good in their own life is not good enough; traditional Buddhists need to challenge the government.

Many governments spend too much money on arms. When governments spend money on arms, it's against the first and the second precept. Even Mr. Eisenhower, who was a five star general when he became the President, said that all money spent on nuclear arms, on big tanks, big battle ships is, in fact, the government stealing money from the public. That money should be spent on public health, education and social welfare. Mr. Eisenhower wasn't Buddhist, nor did he practise as a Christian. But his words are powerful for Buddhist to meditate upon, and we should use them to challenge our government. Unless we challenge the government mindfully and nonviolently, we will be allowing the society to be unjust.

Likewise, sexual misconduct does not only imply the personal affairs, of Mr. Clinton and Ms. Lewinsky. The entire media promotes sexual misconduct. Most of the mainstream media, particularly television and advertisements, are using women's bodies, using lust to seduce people into buying things.

Promoting greed and lying is accepted. Most politicians tell lies. Most advertisements tell lies. Most Buddhists keep their mouth shut. The fifth precept not only refers to alcohol and drugs, but also implies advertisements or ideologies which make people blind or attached to something which is false.

The International Network of Engaged Buddhists was created eleven years ago to link Buddhists together and to work on social and political issues. At the same time they ask Buddhists to practise mindfulness in order to take issues peacefully and non-violently.

The World Fellowship of Buddhists began in the 1950's and has become somewhat of a rich man's club. They meet every 2 years and tell each other how wonderful we Buddhists are. They take no stand on social or political issues because they're so good and so lovely that they are above the world. This is why I emphasize that Buddhists must link together and practise Buddhism internally, yet at the same time work socially and politically. The Buddha taught us to interrelate. So this is one aspect of my work—linking Buddhists together.

The second aspect of my work is ecumenical: the coming together of Buddhist, Christian, Muslim, Hindu, Jew, and those of others traditional indigenous religions, like Shamanism and the spiritual traditions practised by the American Indians, the Mauri, and so on. Those of us who come together feel that there is no hierarchy in religion. It is silly to claim that Buddhism is superior to Christianity or vice versa. That is the old fashion of over one hundred years ago but, unfortunately, is still practised in Korea.

Unless we unite together we will fail because there is now a new demonic religion which everyone, including Buddhist, Christian, and Muslim subscribes to—that is Consumerism. This demonic religion is controlled by multinational corporations which are more powerful than any state including the United States. They control the main media and most of the world products. People like Mr. Murdoch try to control the mainstream media all over the world. People like Mr. Soros try to manipulate money all over the world. United Food Company in the US controls most of the food production in the world. McDonalds controls most of the fast food all over the world. We need not mention Pepsi Cola, Nestle, Coca Cola. They condition us to believe that if we don't buy, if we don't purchase, if we're not fashionable, we are nobody. They reduce human being to the point that there are only two aspects left of human beings—one is born to earn money and then consuming whatever we are told to do so by the advertisements.

Multinational corporations employ the best brains to serve them. They have the best, most advanced, and expensive technology. Yet they are controlled by greed. Wherever there is any natural resource they want to use it up. These corporations will capitalize on cheap labor, yet they have no moral legitimacy and no spiritual insight. If religious traditions unite together and come back to our spiritual understanding and moral legitimacy, we can confront them. Unfortunately, most of us in religious traditions lack the spiritual insight and many of our religious leaders are immoral. So we have to revive morality within our religious tradition, and we must dig deeply into our spiritual roots. Then we can unite to work in a positive way as an alternative to consumerism.

My late teacher, Bhikkhu Bhuddhadasa, said as Buddhists, "we must study and practise only the best in Buddhism. Secondly, we must respect our friends' religions. With good friends who practise the best in our religion and good friends in other religions, we must unite together against consumerism, capitalism and all aspects of materialism." Some of us have been working towards that aim for a few years. Last December we had a big gathering outside Bangkok with people from many religious traditions coming together. Unless we have an alternative to consumerism, we cannot overcome this new demonic religion.

To reiterate, my primary work is among Buddhists internationally. My secondary work is more ecumenical, which includes all religious traditions plus nonbelievers, who have common ground against the new demonic religion. My third area of concentration is mostly in my country. It is called Spirit in Education Movement (SEM). I feel, and most of my peers in mainstream education feel, that traditional education has now come to an end because mainstream education is following the west blindly. In the West people are taught to develop their head; they do not develop their heart. Hence the clever one needs not be good; that's the first drawback. The second drawback is that in the West, people have been taught to develop intellectually and compartmentally, in a dualistic manner. Natural scientists and social scientists do not understand each other. Engineers and medical doctors do not understand each other. In each discipline expertise is developed to such an extent that you miss the wood for the tree. Western medical scientists treat the patient as if it were mechanical: some medical doctors only deal with the brain, while others only treat the heart or the skin.

Tibetan medicine deals with the patient in four ways. Firstly, the patient has either a right or wrong view. Having the right view one is healthy; having the wrong view one is less healthy. Having the right view implies not wanting to be greedy, not wanting to be powerful, not wanting to exploit other people—obviously one will be more healthy. Secondly, it depends on one's Karma; if one did unskillful things in the past, the results will be experienced in the present. The past need not be a past life, it may be this life. It effects on your present situation. Thirdly, it depends on one's breathing. If one breathes properly, it helps the lungs, liver, and all one's internal organs. Disease is only the fourth element relating to one's health. Western medicine deals only with disease.

Most colleges and universities produce students in order to get a job—that's all. Economic prosperity has been the incentive in mainstream education; one's salary determines whether one has been successful or not. Thanks to the economic collapse, perhaps mainstream education should now be renounced because the outcome is that most students will be unemployed. My views are shared by most of my peers in mainstream education in the US., the UK., Japan, and many other places.

The Spirit in Education Movement is linked with alternative education in other countries like Naropa Institute in the US, and Schumacher College and Sharpham College in the UK. We encourage students to use breathing as a main element for knowing him or herself. They should learn to empower themselves and then learn to respect others. "Others" here means not only human beings, but includes animals, trees, earth, oceans, rivers, and the whole natural environment. Hierarchy in education, primary school, secondary school, tertiary education, higher degrees and so on are all rubbish imposed by the West.

Three years ago we experimented with a course on Buddhist development in contrast to western development. This first course was conducted for only three weeks. A professor attened from Germany, a doctor and students from the UK; we had illiterate Thai peasant, and monks and nuns from Laos and Cambodia—about forty of us together in three weeks, with interpreters of course. We studied in natural surroundings just like Santiniketan. We learned from each other. The doctor from Germany learned from the farmer from Laos. The farmer from Laos learned from the British and so on. We all became teachers, students and friends and we went to places where Thai Buddhist monks had hospices for those dying with HIV. We visited places where Cambodian Buddhist monks empowered people who lost all hope, who had been drug addicted. Through meditation practice they overcame this and they now have cooperative movement, having developed a rice bank and buffalo bank, both of which have been very effective.

The Spirit in Education Movement is three years old. We now have students from America and England coming to us for 3-6 week courses, exposing themselves to suffering, to meditation in the jungle, and so on. Right now we are training indigenous tribal people from Burma, thirty of them, for three months at our place.

The International Network of Engaged Buddhists, the ecumenical work on Alternative to Consumerism, and the Spirit in Education Movement have been linked all over the world. However, we are quite weak in our link with Korea. If my talk today has been beneficial, I hope we will have more Korean friends working with us hand in hand.

17 November 1998

ON THE INDICATORS OR CRITERIA OF DEVELOPMENT FROM A BUDDHIST POINT OF VIEW

It is difficult to see how religious philosophical categories could be easily transformed into criteria for development. However, let us try to find some criteria which could be considered as indicators of development from a Buddhist point of view. The main intention of this paper is to specify how, according to Buddhist philosophy, the ultimate goal in life is for the human being to reach its fullest potential.

First of all, one criterion could be *the involvement of all interested subjects into a process of development*. This is based on the idea of the interdependence of everything and everyone. According to this view, it could be concluded that qualitative development is possible only with the inclusion of as many subjects as possible into the very process of development.

Secondly, continuing the logic that everything is interdependent, another criterion of qualitative development is the understanding that *any development today cannot be at the expense of any human being, community or country*.

Thirdly, Buddhist religion teaches that *there cannot be any development based on passion: on hatred, violence, and greed*. So if there is an economy or economic development which is based to a great extent on the gambling industry, this phenomenon could not be called "a development."

Fourthly, the *concept of sharing* is very strong in Buddhist philosophy. In a broad sense, it means sharing love, compassion and also sharing one's sufferings. If a favorable environment is created for the *flourishment of philanthropy*, and a *good social security net system* is introduced, then this society could be considered a developed society.

Fifthly, if one continues developing the concept of sharing, one inevitably comes to the problem of setting up a *good tax system where there is a just sharing of profit*. According to this logic, a tax system which allows a single person (or a small community) to accumulate so much profit (wealth) that it is much more than necessary for the demands of that person or the community, that tax system should be adjusted according to the notion of sharing.

Sixthly, *killing* of any living creature is considered to be an unwholesome action in Buddhism. One could come to the conclusion that any economy directed at the production of weapons of mass destruction, *any society with uncontrolled military expenditures could be considered an economy leading to destruction*.

Seventhly, Buddhist philosophy is very much concerned with keeping *the purity of body, speech, and mind*. Therefore, development which is friendly to the environment (body or outer conditions), the mind (human beings or inner condition), and the speech (the means of development) is a qualitative one.

Eighthly, it is interesting to observe the close connection which exists between a *means* of development and the ultimate *goal* of development. An effective goal is only achieved through and by positive means. This, then, is the criterion of *the connection of a positive means with a beneficial goal*. Any attempt to achieve a good goal by unskillful means (violence, victims, and so on) could not and should not be considerd as development.

Ninethly, the term "development" is possible after a human being or a community has reached a certain level of living. For instance, in Buddhism a person really "develops" only after he/she starts hearing and practising the teachings of the Buddha.

A nation "develops" only after it solves the problem of hunger, and war. Otherwise no one (nation/country) understands what is meant by qualitative development. *Development starts where hunger, war, and extreme poverty finishes, which is where the observation of basic human rights (right to live, right to express oneself), and the dignity of human beings begins.*

Reflections on Buddhism and Development
by Sulak Sivaraksa and colleagues, Thailand

[from World Faiths and Development, papers from the World Bank, World Religions meeting at Lambeth Palace, London, February 1998, published by World Faiths Development Dialogue, October 1998.]

SULAK SIVARAKSA IN SIAM

Our series of Bodhi advisers continues with Sulak Sivaraksa, who was educated as a barrister in England and taught as a guest lecturer in the US at the University of California at Berkeley and Cornell University. As an outspoken human and environmental rights activist in Siam (which he prefers to Thailand), Sulak has faced exile and public burning of his numerous books. Sulak has been nominated twice for the Nobel Prize for Peace and received the prestigious Right Livelihood Award in 1995. Some of the following has been extracted from an interview by Tom Welsh with Sulak, published recently in the *Korea Herald*; some comes from our personal knowledge.

21st Century Activism

Sulak, educated in both East and West, exemplifies Buddhism in action. Though deeply steeped in Buddhist philosophy, and an advocate for both the renewal of Buddhism and its adaptation to the modern world, Sulak believes that meditation alone is insufficient. He is critical of complacent Western meditators who "meditate to achieve inner peace and a comfortable life". Sulak argues that "Buddhism compels us to confront suffering, to recognise the structure of evil in the world and to oppose it through non-violent means". His activism ranges over a wide field, including alternative economics, education, care for the dying and conservation.

Sulak has been involved in the formation and operation of Alternatives to Consumerism (ATC), Spirit in Education Movement (SEM) and the International Network of Engaged Buddhists (INEB).

I buy, therefore I am

Sulak expresses the ethos of consumerism by paraphrasing Descartes' famous words, "I think, therefore I am". He believes that consumerism and economic globalisation have undermined traditional spiritual values and widened the gap between Asia's rich and poor. Sulak's Alternatives to Consumerism (ATC) argues that we must confront the new consumerism in order to maintain community-based values. ATC organises gatherings so that people from diverse communities may exchange stories and share experiences, a foil to the mass media that so actively promotes consumerism.

While some may see Sulak's economic agenda as overly idealistic, he believes that these ideas are viewed with increasing sympathy by international policy-makers. He describes the recently appointed President of the World Bank, Australian James Wolfensohn, as "very well-intentioned" and observes that "in some ways, the World Bank seems to be coming around." Sulak noted the World Bank's support of a program he launched that is designed to teach peasant farmers appropriate technology. He cautions, "It will take more than gestures to relieve the unbearable suffering of the poor in Asia... a fundamental change in outlook on the part of Western policy-makers [is needed]. And that's very difficult". Benevolent Organisation for Development, Health & Insight (BODHI) focuses on sustainable ways to improve health, education, the environment and human rights, particularly in developing countries. BODHI was founded in 1989 on the principles of skilful and compassionate action.

BODHI is neither religious nor political. We have supporters and advisers from many faiths. We ask for a kind heart and practical assistance.

Realising the interdependence of all beings is in our enlightened self-interest. If we don't work together to reduce the world's much-discussed problems, then who will?

[from *Bodhi Times*, December, 1998, No.15 Tasmania, Australia.]

THE YEAR AHEAD : At a Crossroads

1999 is a year that holds great potential for change. This of course could be positive or negative change. The economic crisis and the subsequent attempts at reform have created an unstable atmosphere. Instability, especially in the Buddhist sense is a prime opportunity for the flourishing of wisdom. Both in the sense that it is the place where one confronts impermanence and learns to be more reflective and flexible instead of always falling on the "party line". And in another way, when things are falling apart we look to our own culture's wisdom traditions and leaders to reconstruct society based on healthier more sustainable paradigms.

However, instability, which we will undoubtedly continue to face in 1999, can be used by those who do not have the people's best interests at heart, those who are greedy and insecure, to try and grab all they can. We saw much corruption come to light in 1998 and I think that if we continue down the same path, 1999 will be the year of corruption. Many politicians and other officials will try to insulate themselves against any further crisis by lining their pocketbooks or using the instability to consolidate political power. Some will try to feed off of the aid packages, which they will promote even though they are not in the nation's best interests.

From the outlook of the Siamese people, 1999 is shaping up to be a year of opportunity and challenges also. The economic crisis has and will continue to put people out of their jobs. It is creating hard times for the farmers and fishermen and it is teaching the Thai middle class a lesson about what brings real, true contentment. When your Mercedes is repossessed or you lose a high paying high stress job, maybe there is finally time to spend with the family or at the Wat learning or building community spirit. There are signs that the middle class is awakening to fight for social justice just like they did in 1992. For example in Kanchanaburi the local merchants and other middle class people banded together to fight against the Yadana pipeline. They did so not for their own benefit, but because they are concerned about the human rights of their Burmese neighbors, and the people who live in the forest, also the elephants, the trees, and the rivers. From Kanchanaburi, the trend is spreading. In Krabi the middle class are joining together to oppose the filming of the movie, The Beach. And in Chiang Mai the people are very keen now to help the hill tribes people who are, in effect, their neighbors. This is a very hopeful sign, if the middle class becomes more concerned about social justice and the poor continue to organize and voice their opinion with confidence we will really see positive changes in 1999. The students too are awakening. They have been taught to go to school just so you can get a job, don't worry about education, wisdom or compassion. But now they see, even if they do all they are told, they still don't get a job. So now many students are working for human rights, for the environment and they are also going back to the Wat to find out the meaning and the benefit of community service.

In 1999 the poor will be faced with choices in reacting to these hard times. My hope is that they will continue to organize and to struggle for their rights over their livelihood resources—peacefully and nonviolently of course, but with determination. The danger of 1999 is that the IMF and corrupt government officials either forcibly deny people their rights or trick them in the name of economic reform/recovery, into selling their way of life for a few thousand baht. What happens then? More farmers' daughters sold into prostitution, more farmers work as laborers on the land their family had owned for generations, or they move to Bangkok to live in the slum and work in the factory.

The turbulence of 1999 is sure to cause conflict. If we, the people are not vigilant it might be the year our country is sold or stolen from under our own noses. Perhaps corrupt politicians will do it or the army generals taking advantage of the crisis for their personal benefit. If we are not careful the transnational corporations might rule 1999.

My hope is that 1999 is the year that more and more Siamese

people recognize the beauty and contentment inherent in our traditional way of life. I hope that the accelerating trend toward outright westernization and commercialization of Siam is halted. Through organizations like the Forum of the Poor, the farmers can grow stronger and protect their way of life and right to a simple but healthy existence. Groups like the Spirit in Education Movement can keep on helping the Siamese middle class people recognize that spirituality and generosity, not consumerism and greed are the keys to real happiness. It could be a great year or a disastrous year. In any case we are definitely at a crossroads. Which way will we go in 1999, that is up to us!

[from *Bangkok Post*, January 31, 1999.]

THE SKILLFUL MEANS OF
SOCIAL ACTIVISM

Sulak Sivaraksa

A social activist and founder of many initiatives which seek to combat consumer values and promote spiritually-based development, Sulak's work has repeatedly brought him repression from the Thai authorities. He founded the *Social Science Review* that soon became the most influential publication in Thailand; he created a string of social welfare and development organizations; he is largely credited with the famous Jungle University for fleeing Burmese students, and has developed a new college in Thailand: the Spirit in Education Movement.

Social Activism

Concern for human democracy, human rights and accountable government has been the main thrust of my life and work. I am outspoken in my beliefs and as a result, from time to time, I have had to go into exile to escape arrest or to gaurantee my safety. I have also been in jail as a consequence of my outspokenness against the Thai Government and the way it treats the Thai people. In 1963 I founded the *Social Science Review* which played a crucial role in stimulating student awareness, prior to the 1973 uprising when the military regime was overthrown. The government has now come to realize that they must tolerate outspokenness, they must listen to the truth, and that what I and others have been trying to do through non-violence is of great value. This year, army and police officers have come to study non-violent techniques, which is wonderful.

I consider myself an engaged Buddhist, one who is involved

with social activism from a Buddhist perspective. In traditional Buddhism we care for our own well-being—physical, mental, and spiritual—as well as the well-being of others, of society. Buddhism advocates the basic principle of non-violence or *ahimsa*. It is not easy to maintain an attitude of non-violence when there is rape, murder, and child abuse all around you. We need more seeds of peace. After 1988 many Burmese students were killed, others fled to the Thai border. They were full of violence. I made friends with them and built trust and then I was able to offer them something skillful. We established the Jungle University for Burmese refugee students so they may continue their education. Certainly they wanted to raise arms, they wanted to fight. But some have come to understand the non-violent approach. The more you confront issues it doesn't help. Twenty five years ago many Thai students were killed, they were betrayed. Now, many of them realize the principle of *ahimsa* is deeply powerful.

I felt .that such consumerism and violence is dominating the world. We must be able to challenge this unjust social structure non-violently, to become more indigenous, to care for our own community. We have developed many social welfare organizations in Siam to really help people in the way they need it. All people question the role of non-violence, and say that in some circumstances we have to be violent. Nelson Mandela has spoken how he felt it becomes immoral to pursue a policy of non-violence as it simply allows the suppressor to pursue. To be honest, I cannot say that non-violence is the only answer. But neither can I vouch for violence. For me, violence has a much worse outcome than non-violence. I remember my American Quaker friends who went to Hanoi during the Vietnam war, and the Vietnamese said to them, "How can we use non-violence when you people are bombing us like this?" There is no answer to this. I simply could not be violent, it would go against everything in my being. Someone may say it's escapism, but I could not justify it morally.

If one is limited in resources and time, how can one apply social activism? What things can one do that would have the greatest effect? I think change happens when we see somebody who is truly suffering. Then, I think we would change our lifestyle, we would see how we can be less materialistic, how we can take less and give more. It is not right to accumulate wealth while people are homeless and suffering. When you make your lifestyle simpler it has a great meaning. We feel the more we acquire the more we will be happy, but that is not the case.

This means starting from one's own insight. If one is peaceful, if one is harmonious with oneself, then one will see things in the proper light, as they really are. If one doesn't have that insight, one is bound to be unskillful, to cause harm. There is an important teaching in the terms skillful and unskillful. If we are not clear in our vision then what we do will ultimately be for our own egoistic needs. Many of us do things in the name of social justice, in the name of ideology, but unskillfully, without awareness or sensitivity. That is bound to hurt both ourselves and others.

I have been involved in helping drug abusers to heal their lives, as well as working with AIDS patients. This has helped me personally, for when I am confronted with drug addicts I am reminded of the impermanence of life. It reminds me that these are fellow sufferers, that we all suffer in life. So, I do anything I can to help them. We feel that medicine alone does not help, especially with AIDS. They need more to help them confront the suffering within themselves. At the same time we use skillful means to show them how to be calm, how to meditate to find peace.

Forgiveness is very important. In order to forgive properly one must cultivate fearlessness. When one is fearless, one can forgive, yet we are full of fear. One has to empower oneself spiritually, otherwise one forgives only with one's words. One can forgive an action with words, but it still remains in one's heart and one's mind. If one really wants to forgive, this is where deep meditation practice is essential. Aung San Suu Kyi was put under house arrest and she forgave her oppressors. She said, "I have no fear." It is the same with the Americans who went back to Vietnam to help their former enemies. Through these kind of actions forgiveness becomes beautiful. Then I think we become a full human being. I don't forgive easily, especially governments, but one good thing about being old is eventually I do forgive. My wife says I have become much more effective now because I use less violent words! Although I have never been violent, I now use softer words. I try to praise people rather than blame them, to see what is right rather than what is wrong.

If I don't forgive then it stays in me. Forgiveness is really selfish; you feel so much better when you forgive. Ultimately you must cultivate loving-kindness and compassion for your enemy. Then you see how we are all inter-related. I try to reserve certain times of the day to be quiet. To breathe, to feel forgiveness and compassion. As a Buddhist, I hope eventually to reach Nirvana, but since I have not yet reached that ultimate state, I try to reach Nirvana at least every few moments; to be peaceful, to be clear of all defilements. When one is engaged in social activism, if one doesn't have true peace of mind, then one's egoistic tendencies will creep in. One gets involved because one wants to be recognized. Sometimes one will get hurt because people may blame one when things do not go well. So we have to be skillful, to be understanding and forgiving. To bring more peace into our lives and into the world, we must think more of creating a compassionate way of life that does not bring pain.

My solution for those who want to make a difference is very simple. Everyone should spend at least 5 or 10 minutes every day breathing deeply. I think that would make a huge difference, because breathing is the most important element in our lives, yet we have so little serious consideration of breathing. One doesn't have to believe in Buddhism or even have to believe in anything. If one is Christian, then breathe Christ into oneself. One feels peace; then breathe out with compassion and love. I think that is essential. For those who can take time to breathe, then I would also say make time to meditate, in whatever spiritual tradition is right for you. In contemplation we can see the people who are suffering and can understand that they are as important as we are. Then, I think some seeds are planted, not only for them, but for our own benefit, as this brings very meaningful change.

[To be published in another book, together with other Buddhist activists like A.T.Ariyaratne of Sri Lanka.]

Prayer of Peace and Meditation

Let us pray for World Peace, social justice and environmental balance which begins with our own breathing.

I breathe in calmly and breathe out mindfully.

Once I have seeds of peace and happiness within me, I try to reduce my selfish desire and reconstitute my consciousness. With less attachment to myself I try to understand the stuctural violence in the world.

Linking my heart with my head, I perceive the world wholistically, full of living beings who are all related to me.

I try to expand my understanding with love to help build a more non-violent world.

I vow to live simply and offer myself to the oppressed.

By the grace of the Compassionate Ones and with the help of good friends, may I be a partner in lessening the suffering of the world so that it may be a proper habitat for all sentient beings to live in harmony during the next millennium.

Sulak Sivaraksa
[from *Prayers for a New Millennium*
edited by Elias Amidon & Elizabeth Roberts, 1999.]

"Poor Siamese! They have been poorly rewarded, always welcoming foreigners, among the peoples of Oriental Asia, the only ones favorably disposed towards the Europeans! In spite of its external problems, the ancient Kingdom of the White Elephant has fully entered into the orbit of Western civilization."

from *Gustave Rolin-Jaequemyns and the Making of Modern Siam*
by Walter E.J. Tips, 1996, p.179.

"The crucial role of Europe's mastery of the means and culture of violence is substantiated by contemporary scholarship. The inhabitants of Asia and the Western Hemisphere were 'appalled by the all-destructive fury of European warfare,' military historian Geoffrey Parker observes: 'It was thanks to their military superiority, rather than to any social, moral or natural advantage, that the white peoples of the world managed to create and control' their 'global hegemony' ... 'Europe's incessant wars' were responsible for 'stimulating military science and spirit to a point where Europe would be crushingly superior to the rest when they did meet,' historian V.G. Kiernan comments aptly. ...

"The review of the planning record that follows might be faulted for keeping too close to the surface, ignoring the deeper roots of policy. That is fair enough. Policy flows from institutions, reflecting the needs of power and privilege within them, and can be understood only if these factors are recognized, including the case now under examination.

'Every age of human history," Adam Smith argued with some justice, reveals the workings of 'the vile maxim of the masters of mankind': 'All for ourselves, and nothing for other People.' The 'masters of mankind' in the half-millenium of the European conquest included Europe's merchant-warriors, the industrialists and financiers who followed in their path, the supranational corporations and financial institutions that are creating what the business press now calls a 'new imperial age,' and the various forms of state power that have been mobilized in their interests. The process continues today as new governing forms coalesce to serve the needs of the masters in a 'de facto world government': the IMF, World Bank, G-7, GATT and other executive agreements. "Institutional structures guided by the vile maxim tend naturally towards two-tiered societies: the masters with their agents, and the rabble who either serve them or are superfluous. State power commonly perpetuates these distinctions, a fact stressed again by Adam Smith, who condemned mercantilism and colonialism as harmful to the people of England generally, but of great benefit to the 'merchants and manufacturers' who were the 'principal architects' of policy. State policy often incurs great social costs, but with rare exceptions, the interests of the 'principal architects' are 'most peculiary attended to,' as in this case. The lesson holds as we move on to the modern era, often applying, in an internationalized economy, even after military defeat. Consider, for example, how the interests of the Nazi collaborators in the corporate and financial worlds were 'most peculiarly attended to' as the US occupation restored them to their proper place.

"In the 'new imperial age,' trade is increasingly becoming a form of centrally-managed interchange, guided by a highly 'visible hand' within particular Transnational Corporations, phenomena of great importance in themselves, which also bear on the ideological trappings. World Bank economists Herman Daly and Robert Goodland point out that in prevailing economic theory, 'firms are islands of central planning in a sea of market relationships.' 'As the islands get bigger,' they add,'there is really no reason to claim victory for the market principle'—particularly as the islands approach the scale of the sea, which departs radically from free market principles, and always has, because the powerful will not submit to these destructive rules."

from *Rethinking Camelot: JFK, the Vietnam War, and U.S. political culture* by Noam Chomsky, South End Press, Boston, 1993.

"Siam was the official name for Thailand 1855-1939 and again 1946-1949. The term is thought to be derived from sayam (dark brown people) or shyama (golden or heavily built) as used by the Mon and Khmer people to describe the Tai-speaking settlers in the Chao Phraya valley. Prime Minister Phibul Songkhram (1938-44 and again 1948-57), a strident nationalist, changed the country's name to 'Prathet Thai' in 1939, generally translated as the 'land of the free.' This was part of a program of modernization and strengthening of Thai patriotism, though his edict to switch to Western-style clothes went against the grain for some patriots. Today some nationalists, one of the most prominent being social critic Sulak Sivaraksa, favor changing the name back to Siam. They feel that 'Thailand' is a somewhat artificial construction."

from *Asiaweek*
Vol.24, No.38, September 25, 1998, p.86.

LIST OF BOOKS DISTRIBUTED BY
SUKSIT SIAM CO.,LTD.

113-115 Fuang Nakhon Rd.,Opp. Wat Rajbopith, Bangkok 10200, Thailand.
Tel. (662) 2259531-2 Fax: (662) 2225188

1. **Angkarn Kalyanapong: A Contemporary Siamese Poet.**   (US$ 5)
   By Angkarn Kalyanapong (Editor: Michael Wright), 82 Pages
2. **Dhammic Socialism.**   (US$ 6)
   By Buddhadasa Bhikkhu, Chief translator and editor Donald K. Swearer,
   Thai Inter-Religious Commission for Development Bangkok 1986,
   142 Pages
3. **Radical Conservatism.**   paperback (US$ 40)
   A volume in celebration of Buddhadasa Bhikkhu's 84th year writtenby e.g.
   Thich Nhat Hanh, Gabriel Lafitte, Phra Debvedhi, Bhikkhu Sumedho,
   Lewis R. Lancaster, Sulak Sivaraksa, John A. McConnell, G. Lubsantseren
   and David W. Chappell etc, 576 Pages
4. **Modern Thai Monarchy and Cultural Politics.**   (US$ 15)
   Edited by David Streckfuss, Santi Pracha Dhamma Institute, 180 Pages
5. **The Dissolution of the Sparkling Bridge.**   (US$ 10)
   Poem by Frank Finney
6. **Mindful Mediation.**   (US$ 20)
   A hand book for Buddhist peace makers, by John A. McConnell, 385 Pages
   Paperback
7. **Entering the Realm of Reality.**   (US$ 15)
   Towards Dhammic Societies. Edited by Jonathan Watts, Alan Senauke,
   Santikaro Bhikkhu. INEB, 291 Pages
8. **Life Without a Choice.**   (US$ 15)
   By Karuna Kusalasaya; Published by Sathirakoses Nagapradipa Foundation &
   Thai Inter Religious Commission for Development Bangkok 1991, 303 Pages
9. **Essays on Thai Folklore.**   (US$ 15)
   By Phya Anuman Rajadhon (new edition),422 Pages
10. **Popular Buddhism in Siam and Other Essays on**
    Thai Studies.   paperback (US$ 15)
    By Phya Anuman Rajadhon, Thai Inter-Religious Commission for Develop-
    ment/Sathirakoses-Nagapradipa Foundation Bangkok 1986, 216 Pages

By Sulak Sivaraksa: A Controversial Siamese, Thai Inter ñ Religious Commission for Development, Bangkok 1998, 206 Pages

26. **When Loyalty Demands Dissent.** (US$ 20)
Sulak Sivaraksa and the charge of lese majeste in Siam 1991 ñ 993,Santi Pracha Dhamma Institute/ Ashram Wongsanit/Sathirakoses-Nagapradipa Foundation, 350 Pages

27. **Socially Engaged Buddhism for the New Millennium:** hard cover (US$ 60)
in honor of Bhikkhu Payutto's 60th birthday. paper back (US$ 38)
By eminent contemporary Buddhist scholars and activists

Occasional Papers by Santi Pracha Dhamma Institute and Spirit in Education Movement

1. Alternative Development. Price 10.00 US$
   From a Buddhist perspective. By Sulak Sivaraksa.
2. Alternative Development. Price 10.00 US $
   From a Buddhist perspective. SEM course report. By Sulak Sivaraksa.
3. Luong Pho Nan : Building Peace. By Pithaya Wongkun. Price 5.00 US $
   Translated from the original Thai by Joshua J. Prokopy.
4. Deep Ecology Forest Walk 1996, Price 5.00 US $
   or "Not Just Another Walk in the Woods."
   SEM course report. By Annette Dunklin & Jennifer Rain.
5. Buddhism and Human Rights in Siam. Price 5.00 US $
   By Sulak Sivaraksa.
6. Thai Buddhist Responses to the AIDS Crisis. Price 5.00 US $
   By Sulak Sivaraksa.
7. Present Trends of Buddhism in Siam- Price 5.00 US $
   and a Positive Future of the Sangha.
   By Sulak Sivaraksa.
8. Ajarn Noam Chomsky : Professor of Linguistics, Price 5.00 US $
   Social Critic, and Conscience for an Unjust World.
   By Tong Banarak.
9. Applying Gandhi for Alternatives to Consumerism. Price 5.00 US $
   By Sulak Sivaraksa.
10. 3rd Annual SEM Lecture. 29 October 1997. Price 5.00 US $
    Silpakorn University, Bangkok Thailand.
    By Jakob von Uexkull.
11. Five Awardees from Sathirakoses-Nagapradipa Price 5.00 US $
    and the Komol Keemthong Foundations.
12. Forum of the Poor. Price 5.00 US $
    By Chris Walker and Danny Campbell.

Seeds of Peace : Bound Volumes
Price 20.00 US$ each

1. Vols I & II : 1985-6 (photocopies)
2. Vols III & IV : 1987-8
3. Vols V & VI : 1989-90
4. Vols VII & VIII : 1991-2 (photocopies)
5. Vols IX & X : 1993-4
6. Vols XI & XII : 1995-6
7. Vols XIII & XIV : 1997-8

Publications by Alternative to Consumerism (ATC)
Price 5.00 US $ each

1. Stories of Alternatives to Consumerism in Siam.
2. Participant Information handbook for December 1997 International Gathering.
3. Alternative Politics for Asia : Dialogue between Sulak Sivaraksa & Helena Norberg - Hodge.
4. Alternative Politics for Asia : Chandra Muzaffar, a Muslim perspective.
5. Alternative Politics for Asia : A Christian perspective, an interview with Bishop Labayan.
6. Alternative Politics for Asia : Interview with Walden Bello.

For each title, please add US$5 for postage
Personal cheque in US dollars payable to
Sulak Sivaraksa is accepted.

Suksit Siam
113 Fuang Nakhon Rd.,
Opp. Wat Rajbopith,
Bangkok 10200,
Thailand.
Tel. (662)2259531-2
Fax. (662)2225188
E-mail: sop@ffc.inet.co.th